STUDIES IN ECONOMIC A[...]

This series, specially commissi[...]
Society, provides a guide to the [...]
themes of economic and social history in which advances have
recently been made or in which there has been significant debate.

Originally entitled 'Studies in Economic History', in 1974 the
series had its scope extended to include topics in social history, and
the new series title, 'Studies in Economic and Social History',
signalises this development.

The series gives readers access to the best work done, helps them
to draw their own conclusions in major fields of study, and by
means of the critical bibliography in each book guides them in the
selection of further reading. The aim is to provide a springboard
to further work rather than a set of pre-packaged conclusions or
short-cuts.

## ECONOMIC HISTORY SOCIETY

The Economic History Society, which numbers over 3000
members, publishes the *Economic History Review* four times a year
(free to members) and holds an annual conference. Enquiries about
membership should be addressed to the Assistant Secretary, Economic History Society, Peterhouse, Cambridge. Full-time students
may join at special rates.

# STUDIES IN ECONOMIC AND SOCIAL HISTORY

*Edited for the Economic History Society by L. A. Clarkson*

## PUBLISHED

OTHER TITLES ARE IN PREPARATION

# The Gold Standard and the International Monetary System 1900–1939

*Prepared for*
*The Economic History Society by*

IAN M. DRUMMOND
*Professor of Economics and Vice-Dean,*
*University of Toronto*

MACMILLAN
EDUCATION

First published 1987

Published by
MACMILLAN EDUCATION LTD
Houndmills, Basingstoke, Hampshire RG21 2XS
and London
Companies and representatives
throughout the world

Printed in Hong Kong

British Library Cataloguing in Publication Data
Drummond, Ian M.
The gold standard and the international monetary system 1900–
1939. — (Studies in economic and social history)
1. Gold standard — History — 20th century
I. Title    II. Economic History Society
III. Series
332.4'52'0904    HG297
ISBN 0–333–37208–5

# Contents

# Note on References

References in the text within square brackets relate to the numbered items in the Bibliography, followed, where necessary, by the page numbers in italics, for example [1,7–9].

# Editor's Preface

When this series was established in 1968 the first editor, the late Professor M. W. Flinn, laid down three guiding principles. The books should be concerned with important fields of economic history; they should be surveys of the current state of scholarship rather than a vehicle for the specialist views of the authors, and above all, they were to be introductions to their subject and not 'a set of pre-packaged conclusions'. These aims were admirably fulfilled by Professor Flinn and by his successor, Professor T. C. Smout, who took over the series in 1977. As it passes to its third editor and approaches its third decade, the principles remain the same.

Nevertheless, times change, even though principles do not. The series was launched when the study of economic history was burgeoning and new findings and fresh interpretations were threatening to overwhelm students — and sometimes their teachers. The series has expanded its scope, particularly in the area of social history — although the distinction between 'economic' and 'social' is sometimes hard to recognize and even more difficult to sustain. It has also extended geographically; its roots remain firmly British, but an increasing number of titles is concerned with the economic and social history of the wider world. However, some of the early titles can no longer claim to be introductions to the current state of scholarship; and the discipline as a whole lacks the heady growth of the 1960s and early 1970s. To overcome the first problem a number of new editions, or entirely new works, have been commissioned — some have already appeared. To deal with the second, the aim remains to publish up-to-date introductions to important areas of debate. If the series can demonstrate to students and their teachers the importance of the discipline of economic and social history and excite its further study, it will continue the task so ably begun by its first two editors.

*The Queen's University of Belfast*                L. A. CLARKSON
                                                                *General Editor*

# Introduction

MUCH of the scholarly work on the gold standard and the international financial system has been additive and revisionist. Thus for the past quarter-century or more, scholars have been building up a mosaic, ever more complicated and realistic, of the way in which the gold standard operated. This pamphlet is therefore concerned primarily to describe that picture. Furthermore, in so far as controversies can indeed be found, they cover only a small portion of the territory. This is especially noticeable in that the monetary literatures of the several countries have developed along rather different lines, so that the controversies of one land may have no parallel in other places. Also, to understand what is at issue in the several controversies one needs an adequate map; experience suggests that on this topic, at least, students can sometimes be so desperately confused about fundamentals that the professional refinements are altogether lost on them. The economic and intellectual terrain of the gold-standard world is so remote from our own that there is immense risk of such confusion. For instance, North American students are so accustomed to associate 'sterling' with silver tableware that they have trouble seeing the pound sterling as a gold-based currency. Therefore it has seemed better to give more space to narrative, and less to controversy, which the interested reader can in any event pursue with the aid of the bibliography. Some of the crucial articles and excerpts from longer works are reproduced in [30].

# 1 The International Gold Standard System before the First World War

THIS chapter treats the international monetary system from 1900 to 1914. A fuller treatment, which covers the entire period 1870–1914, may be found in the eighth volume of the *Cambridge Economic History of Europe* [67]. During these years most of the world's trading countries were said to be 'on the gold standard'. A drift toward gold had begun in 1871, when the new German Empire adopted the gold standard. Yet although the United States made provision for the gold-convertibility of its paper currency in 1879 it adhered firmly to gold only in 1900, with the passage of the Gold Standard Act; even then there were important states, such as China, which from a variety of viewpoints were not members of the system. The result can properly be called a 'gold standard system', in so far as the arrangements of the several countries fitted together in a reasonably coherent way, even though no one had consciously designed it, and even though no international agency administered it, assisted it, or brooded about it. Each country did what it liked, taking its own decisions about monetary matters.

We begin with definitions. We then proceed to analyse the system's workings, concerning ourselves chiefly with three questions: What mechanisms kept so many exchange rates fixed, or almost fixed, for very extended periods? What were the structural characteristics of the international economy which are relevant for our understanding of the monetary system? What techniques did monetary authorities use for the management of the foreign exchanges?

## (i) WHAT WAS THE GOLD STANDARD?

In any one country the gold-standard arrangements derived from law, and sometimes from custom, peculiar to that country.

Although the legal and institutional arrangements were immensely varied, certain common elements were always or almost always present in those countries which were said to be 'on gold'. First and most obviously, the nation's standard money was given a fixed value in terms of gold. This was said to be the 'gold content' of that money – pound, dollar, ruble, franc, mark or whatever. These gold values were the results of historical accident. For instance, the gold content of the pound sterling derived from the silver content of the shilling, the market price of gold in terms of silver in 1717, and the Carolingian definition of a unit of account wherein a pound contained twenty shillings. No one asked whether gold values were consistent with national or international economic equilibrium, however that might be defined. Usually there were actual gold coins, whose mint weights correctly reflected the nominal gold contents, although in some gold-standard countries, such as Russia and Canada, gold coins were rarely encountered. Other metals, such as silver or copper, were coined as well, but these other coins were usually not unlimited 'legal tender' — that is to say, there was usually a limit to the size of obligation that could be settled by offering copper pennies, silver dimes or whatever.

There were admittedly some exceptions. In Germany until 1907, and in France and some smaller European countries, certain silver coins were unlimited legal tender. Elsewhere, however, that status was reserved for gold.

In gold-standard countries there were many sorts of money — bank notes, government paper currency, gold coin, other metallic coins and deposits in the banking system, the array and the mix varying from one nation to another. The volume of gold coin was considerable: in 1913, the circulation of gold coin in Europe, the Americas, the British Empire and Japan was estimated to be 4,100 million American dollars, while the gold reserves in the same territories summed to $4,900 million. In Europe, thanks to the British, the French and the Germans, the ratio of gold in circulation to reserves was substantially larger: $2,400 million in gold circulation, as against $2,100 million in reserves [62; 71, *Tables H1, H2*]. Yet all the gold-standard countries had plentiful experience with paper currency, and there were many arrangements for regulating its issue. There was no standard pattern, and in some countries, such as the United Kingdom, Canada, the United States and Germany, there were several issuing authorities. Sometimes, but by no means always, there was a mechanical relationship between the quantity of circulating paper currency and the quantity of gold in the hands of the issuing authority, which might be a government, a central bank such as the Bank of England, or a commercial bank such as the Bank of Scotland or the Bank of Montreal. The paper currency was supposed to be convertible into gold coin or bullion, on demand, in unlimited amounts, at a fixed price. Thus a hundred-pound bank note, or a hundred pounds in bank deposits, could always be exchanged for a hundred gold sovereigns, giving the paper pound an assured value in terms of gold. Because the Banque de France and until 1907 the Reichsbank had the option of paying silver, this could not quite be said of the franc or the mark. Nor could it be said of the countries such as China, which still adhered to a silver standard, or of countries such as Spain or Austria-Hungary, where the monetary authorities were not committed to pay out metal at all. Thus the Spanish peseta was said to be 'inconvertible paper', even though the holder of pesetas could freely buy other monies, thus indirectly acquiring command over gold — but not at a fixed price.

(ii)   THE GOLD STANDARD AND EXCHANGE RATES

Besides the gold-convertibility we have just described, of equal importance was another kind of convertibility. In peacetime everyone was entirely free to move money, gold or other valuables across national borders, and to convert one national money into another. There was, in other words, no exchange control — no government regulations of transactions in foreign monies. Such freedom, which had not always existed, was not strictly speaking part of the gold standard itself. But for the working of the international gold-standard system this second sort of convertibility was as important as the first. It was the possibility of moving gold, of freely buying and selling all monies, and of converting paper currency freely into gold, which controlled exchange rates.

The comparative gold contents, or relative gold values, established the normal or basic exchange rates, which were usually called 'mint pars', 'gold pars' or 'par values'. Because the pound's gold content was just over 486 per cent of the dollar's, the par value of the pound had to be just over $4.86. However, it was not costless to convert paper into gold, or to ship gold across national borders. Hence the actual exchange rate, as determined by supply and demand, could stand a little higher or a little lower than the par value. Then as now, the vast majority of international transactions came to be settled not by shipping gold, but by buying and selling foreign exchange. Yet the freedom to move money, coin or bullion ensured that actual exchange rates could never move very far from par. The range of variation was defined by what were called the 'gold points'. The 'gold export point' is the exchange rate at which it becomes profitable to ship gold, rather than buy some other money on the foreign exchange market; the 'gold import point' is the rate at which foreigners find it profitable to do likewise. Consider transactions between the pound sterling and the Canadian dollar. Britain's gold export point will be Canada's gold import point, and conversely.

Merchants and businessmen generally thought they knew where the gold points were. But these points were not fixed and immutable. Circumstances — changes in interest rates, transport and insurance costs, and the actions of such responsible monetary authorities as the Bank of England and the Banque de France — could widen or narrow the spread. Morgenstern has argued [75], on the basis of what some observers think rather slender information, that exchange rates seem to have moved outside the gold points from time to time. But his findings simply tell us that the actual gold points were not always the commonly accepted ones which the financial press would publish and sometimes discuss. The results may also suggest that business folk were not always so fast to respond, by obtaining gold and shipping it, as the schematic description implies. Nevertheless, no one denies that exchange rates were confined within quite narrow ranges of fluctuation, year after year after year.

It follows that exchange rates could not be instruments of national economic policy. The gold-standard countries did not think of changing their par values, nor had gold contents been fixed originally with any eye to export competitiveness, the balance of payments or any such considerations. Furthermore, in that no one expected par values or gold contents to change, speculation on exchange-rate movements would necessarily be confined within the narrow range of the gold points. It was almost as if the gold-standard world possessed a single international money. Indeed, for many purposes it hardly mattered in what money debts and claims were denominated. With respect to the inconvertible paper countries and the silver-standard countries, circumstances were different: dealing with these countries, traders and investors faced the perplexities, risks and opportunities that have become familiar to traders and financiers in the floating-currency world of the 1970s and 1980s. The gold-standard system did not automatically produce balance of payments equilibrium, or any other sort of happy economic result, such as the absence of uncomfortable fluctuations in prices, profits or employment. Indeed, some countries were chronically in current-account surplus, while others chronically ran deficits: that is to say, their receipts from the exports of goods and services chronically fell short of their earnings from the same sources. The system could and did co-exist with major international financial crises, such as that of 1907. Gold-standard countries did not always find it easy or painless to remain 'on gold': some Latin American states were 'off' as often as they were 'on', and even the mighty Russian Empire, struggling with war and revolution in 1904–5, clung to the gold standard only by the skin of its teeth. Yet other states — most obviously France, Germany, the United States and the United Kingdom — seem to have operated the gold standard with few apparent signs of strain, especially in comparison with later years, although even Britain and the USA had some unusual troubles during the international financial crisis of 1907. For these nations, and for others like them, 'success' might be thought to mean the holding of exchange rates within narrow ranges for extended periods, without having to invoke exchange control. How did they do it?

(iii) THE GOLD STANDARD, THE BALANCE OF PAYMENTS AND PRICES

It would once have been argued that 'they' did not 'do it' at all — that automatic processes in the world economy kept the exchange rates within the gold points, and kept the major states on gold. Such ideas have been in circulation for a very long time, ever since the eighteenth century, when the Scottish savant David Hume first proposed what was later called the 'price-specie-flow mechanism'. This elegant idea, which circulated in the 1920s [21] and which

13

used to turn up in textbooks, suggested that if a country was on the gold standard it could never suffer any sustained loss of gold. Should gold flow out, the money supply would fall, inducing a fall in prices; at the same time, because the rest of the world was gaining gold the external price level would rise. The result would be a reversal of the initial flow, as the rest of the world lost competitiveness while the home country became more competitive. Regrettably, this mechanism cannot be the whole story, and may not even be very much of it. Doubts began in the 1920s, when efforts to test the price-specie-flow hypothesis against the evidence produced rather bad results [96; 98]. Subsequent research, and further refinement of the analytical constructs, have been equally damaging, so that few observers now think the hypothesis tells us anything very useful about what actually happened from week to week or from month to month.

At least three sorts of difficulty have been identified. Adjustments seem to have happened faster than one might have expected; it is far from clear that prices moved far enough, or fast enough, to effect the necessary adjustments, nor were the differences among countries sufficiently pronounced; it has been observed that changes in a nation's holdings of gold or foreign exchange did not necessarily produce any particular change in the domestic money supply. For this there might be several reasons. For one thing, commercial banking was developing rapidly, and although in the long run there would probably be some relation between the growth of domestic currency and deposit liabilities — the main components of the money supply — and the growth of the banks' gold and foreign exchange holdings, in the short run there were generally no legal or commercial considerations which would enforce a close parallel. For another thing, in those comparatively few countries which had central banks, the central bank might well pursue a policy which uncoupled the domestic money and credit situation from gold movements. That is known to have been the case in several gold-standard countries, including France and Russia [3].

It used to be suggested that the workability of the gold standard showed that central banks must have followed the 'rules of the gold standard game' [3]. This was quite a simple idea; it suggested that unless central banks operated their domestic monetary system in accordance with the assumptions of the Hume model, expanding

14

the domestic monetary base when gold flowed in and contracting it when gold flowed out, the gold-standard system would break down, because an inflow of gold might not produce an increase in the money supply, nor would a gold outflow always decrease that supply. It would seem to follow that the success of the gold standard must imply something about adherence to the 'rules'. Regrettably, research has demonstrated [3; 28; 90] that the rules of the game were frequently ignored, and that most though not all central banks had no intention of playing the gold-standard game by any particular rules. Thus, although one must have the rules in mind when studying the monetary histories of the several gold-standard states, they certainly had no general relevance, nor were they 'in force' all the time.

Another sort of automatic servo-mechanism is contained within the income adjustment models which derive in one way or other from the Keynesian economic thought of the 1930s. Such models take various forms, directing our attention to the interconnections among national outputs, imports and exports, in the several nations. They all imply that the process of income-adjustment, which follows on any disturbance to the balance of payments, will restrain and perhaps eliminate any undue outflow or inflow of gold. The more sophisticated models, such as that employed by Ford [36; 37], also allow for interaction between output, employment, the interest rate and capital movements. For some countries, such as Britain, Canada and Argentina, income-adjustment models have increased our understanding of the forces which produced gold movements [37; 67]. But for few countries has there been any serious effort to apply the models to the interpretation of pre-1914 events. Furthermore, with the passage of time Keynesian models have fallen out of fashion among economists, many of whom are distressed by the implicit assumptions on which they rest.

Perhaps it would be reasonable to suppose that the servo-mechanisms were at work 'to some extent' in all countries, so that an element of automatic adjustment was indeed present — working very slowly, but surely, to equilibrate the system of exchange rates in the long run. The most elegant application in the literature is probably that of Ford, who has applied an income-adjustment model to the United Kingdom [36]. Ford argues that although in principle the gold-standard mechanism could impose hardships both for the central countries, such as Britain, and for the peripheral ones, such as Argentina, one must study each crisis to discover what actually did occur. He shows that in general British long-term capital export could be transferred without difficulty because the spending of the proceeds in Britain led first to an increase in Britain's commodity exports, and then to an increase in commodity imports, and in British interest rates, which in turn affected both short-term and long-term movements of capital. Thus in 1907 Britain survived the drain of gold to North America not by pumping funds from the periphery, but by drawing gold from Europe and perhaps from domestic circulation. In this case the adjustment did little damage either on the periphery or in Britain itself; however, other instances might look very different [36, 35–9]. In particular, in other countries the adjustment process might work in quite different ways.

Economists are still constructing new general schemata of the gold standard's working, largely in terms of what is now called the 'monetary approach to the balance of payments' [5; 30; 67; 97]. In this approach it is suggested that gold flows are the results, not the causes, of international adjustment processes. If a gold-standard country needs more money, it is suggested, its balance of payments will adjust in such a way as to attract more gold; conversely, if there is more domestic money than its citizens want to hold, it will lose gold. These schemata are of considerable interest, but it would probably be agreed that as yet no one scheme commands wide acceptance. It seems better to concentrate here upon structural and institutional peculiarities which are very much part of the gold-standard system.

(iv) THE GOLD STANDARD AND THE STRUCTURE OF THE WORLD ECONOMY

There were elements in the structure of the world economy which, although not elegant servo-mechanisms, helped to keep the gold-standard system working. The system could readily accommodate real economic growth at stable or rising price levels only if the quantity of monetary gold, both for coin and for reserves, was rising as well. If the several countries had all been trying to stay on gold, and also to grow in real terms, while competing for an unchanging stock of gold, great stresses would have appeared almost at once. Kitchen has estimated [62] that between 1890 and 1914 the international gold standard required the accumulation of monetary gold worth nearly a thousand million pounds — an immense sum at the time. Fortunately, thanks to new discoveries in South Africa, the United States, the Yukon, Russia and Australia, and thanks to new methods of extracting and refining, between 1890 and 1914 newly mined gold was in ample supply. Of course no country chose to go on the gold standard simply because there was plenty of gold to be had. Indeed, several of the critical decisions were taken in the 1870s, before the new deposits had been discovered: in that decade Germany, France and the United States all adopted the gold standard in one form or another. But the extra gold lubricated the system.

In general, countries which wanted more monetary gold were also running current-account surpluses. Among such states were France, Germany, Holland, Belgium, the United Kingdom and in most years after 1900 the United States. All these countries were exporting capital, largely in long-term forms. By doing so, they supplied the needs of the countries — chiefly Russia, the lands of south-eastern Europe, Latin America and the British Empire — which chronically ran current-account deficits. But because their capital exports normally fell short of their current-account surpluses, newly mined gold tended to flow to them because they were not relending all their current-account surpluses. The monetary gold of the world was very unequally distributed. At the end of 1913 the five great powers of Europe held almost half of it, and the USA held another 22 per cent, leaving less than 30 per cent for the rest of the world — that is, for the territories whose balances of payments were normally in deficit on current account. Hence the suspicion, voiced among others by Ford, that in principle the ease with which the 'central countries', such as Britain, stayed on gold might have been bought at the expense of the peripheral ones, such as Canada or Argentina. In capital-importing countries gold coins were unusual; it was the rich capital exporters which could afford the luxury of a gold circulation. For these countries the coinage was an element of safety: any temporary disruption to the payments position would automatically bring some coins out of circulation and into the banks so that the monetary reserves would be replenished as the money supply went down.

17

If the surplus countries had brought all their surpluses home in the form of gold there would have been very severe strains in the deficit countries — at least until the servo-mechanisms had produced inflation in Western Europe and slump in such lands as Argentina, Canada and India. Thus the system worked fairly smoothly for most debtor countries only because Britain and the other creditor states regularly pumped so much capital out and across their borders. Fortunately for the debtors, most of this capital was supplied in long-term forms which could not readily be pulled back home in time of trouble, whether real or imagined. There has been much discussion about these flows: were they pushed out by conditions in the capital-exporting countries, or pulled out by conditions 'on the periphery' [8; 29; 34; 54]? Sad to relate, these controversies have been so marred by analytical perplexities that it would not be fruitful to report them here. Capital flows might be expected whenever the overseas or foreign returns, adjusted for risk, are no lower than domestic returns. In many of the debtor countries the developments of the period seem to have produced the expectation of higher rates, reflecting new discoveries, local opportunities and government policies. Thus when foreign borrowers came from the rest of the world to seek loans in London, Paris, Berlin or New York, they were willing to offer higher rates, and they generally thought it safe to do so. So long as people remained optimistic about the prospects in a debtor land, the capital flow would continue, redistributing the creditors' surpluses along the lines which the gold standard required.

This is not to say that all was for the best in a Panglossian world even though Bloomfield [3, 44; 4] can find little evidence that the management of central-bank discount rates had painful effects on domestic price levels or unemployment rates. But central banking was almost entirely a European phenomenon. Elsewhere things could go wrong, and sometimes did, especially in Latin America, where failures of confidence were severe, where export earnings did not always rise as expected, and where the domestic political scene was often inimical to any sort of monetary stabilisation [37]. The gold standard generally worked smoothly in the British dominions and in India, at least after 1900. Perhaps things tended to go better in the British Empire because of the external reserves, and the external short-term borrowings, of the commercial banks which operated in the dominions and in the Dependent Empire, and because of the Indian government's London reserves and borrowings. There was also the commitment of local officials and politicians to sound money and sound finance. Indeed, in the self-governing colonies governments did not generally issue paper currency, and where they did, as in Canada, the power was circumscribed by statute. Australia, where the Commonwealth government acquired similar powers in 1910–11, had little chance to experiment with the new device before the outbreak of war. To issue paper currency, or to do so more freely, would require new legislation which a colonial politician might think about twice before introducing. Faced with an unexpected outlay or a revenue-shortfall, he was far more likely to go and borrow in London.

The world monetary system, and therefore the gold standard system, provided for multilateral clearing. That is, balances earned or borrowed in one country could be freely used anywhere else. This was important because the payments between pairs of countries were rarely in bilateral balance. If multilateral clearing had not been possible, some of the strongest countries — including the United Kingdom — would have been in trouble at once, and few countries would have been able to balance their accounts bilaterally [84]. In turn, surpluses could be earned in some directions and deficits incurred in others not only because of the logic of international specialisation and division of labour but because of tariff structures. Britain, for instance, could earn surpluses on her trade with India partly because there was no protective Indian tariff on cottons; meanwhile, Britain's industrial structure and her free trade posture led to immense purchases of cotton, food and tobacco from North America, where American and Canadian protective tariffs made it impossible to sell comparable values of manufactures. Similarly, because Britain was in surplus on current account and because her financial system was well organised, London was an excellent place to raise long-term loans, but the borrowings did not have to be spent in London; they could provide lubrication wherever some oiling was needed.

The need for lubrication, in turn, may have been reduced by the fact that so much of world trade was invoiced in pounds and financed by London, where many overseas banks held transactions balances, where they could obtain short-term credits in case of need, and where so large a proportion of payments was cleared. Within rather narrow limits, private credits from the London mar-

19

ket could help fill temporary needs, so that the market functioned to some limited extent as a lender of last resort for the world monetary system. Furthermore, the clearing of payments, and their multilateral offsetting, must have reduced the need for bilateral exchange transactions which might otherwise have applied pressure to exchange rates and to reserves. These are the things which people have in mind when they say that the pre-1914 gold standard was 'really a sterling standard'.

So much for servo-mechanisms and structural characteristics. For the United States and for the many other states which had no central banks, these were what mattered. For the minority which historical accident had endowed with central banks, policy might also matter, and purposive action was possible, at least in theory, although not always in practice.

(v) NATIONAL MONETARY POLICIES

The central banks of Europe did not co-operate. Indeed, they rarely communicated with one another. The Bank of England, Clapham writes, 'heard from no one; saw no one; only watched the gold and took the necessary steps semi-automatically' [15, *vol. II, 401*; see also 85]. Bloomfield [3] has wondered how automatic the central banks' behaviour really was. But he has raised no question about their remoteness, which, indeed, is not surprising: attempts at international monetary co-operation in the 1860s and 1870s had not led very far, and European bankers, including central bankers, are traditionally a secretive lot. This is not to say that there was no consultation, especially in crises, or that central banks never helped one another. In the troubles of 1906–7, for instance, the Banque de France bought short-term assets in London, thus supplying that market with gold. Such help, however, was the exception not the rule.

Neither the Bank of England nor the United Kingdom government took much interest in the health, welfare, stability or continuance of the international gold-standard system. But the Bank was very much concerned with protecting the gold standard for Britain herself. The Bank did not hold very much gold, and most of its holdings were immobilised because they were needed under the Bank Act of 1844 in 'support' of the paper-currency issue.

Thus unless that issue was to be reduced what mattered was 'free gold' — the gold not thus immobilised — which the Bank called the 'Reserve'. When this was uncomfortably low, or falling, the Bank was almost certain to raise Bank Rate, the basic rate at which it stood willing to lend to the market. Between the beginning of 1900 and the outbreak of war, Bank Rate was changed 71 times. It was thought at the time, and afterwards, that Bank Rate was a weapon of immense power, able to pull gold from the ends of the earth. However, the Bank did not rely on it alone. Through what Americans would later call 'open market operations' it could enter the money market on its own initiative, buying and selling assets so as to affect the level and structure of interest rates. It could and sometimes did vary the price at which it would deal in gold bars and foreign gold coins, or it could provide cheap loans for gold-importers; these measures, which are called the 'gold devices', had the effect of changing the gold points. Finally, the Bank could negotiate special arrangements with some of its larger customers, especially the India Office and the Bank of Japan. But chiefly it relied on the management of Bank Rate.

Why did Bank Rate work so well? It would seem that the Bank of England neither knew nor cared, but later scholars have found the matter very thought-provoking [85; 86; 97], partly because other centres were not always so successful or so comfortable, and partly because in these other centres interest rates so often moved upward and downward along with Bank Rate. Thus except in relation to France, an upward movement of Bank Rate rarely produced a permanent or long-sustained widening of the interest-rate differential in favour of London [64]. But other central banks would respond only after a delay, and even a short delay could produce an inward flow of funds fully sufficient to satisfy the Bank, perhaps by retaining a portion of the weekly gold shipments from South Africa. Nor would funds leave if other central banks raised their rates only enough to compensate for the Bank's initial increase.

A quite different line of argument relies on the presumption that London's short-term claims on the rest of the world were considerably larger than the world's short-term claims on London. Whenever Bank Rate rose London became a more profitable place to hold funds and a more expensive place to owe them; not only would short-term balances flow in, at least until other monetary centres raised their rates, but some overseas debtors would let their obligations run off, producing a net inward movement of short-term funds through the reduction in short-term claims on the rest of the world. Once again, a small change in the net position could well be enough to satisfy the Bank. But although the data are far from satisfactory, both Lindert [64] and Bloomfield [4] have cast doubt on the argument: Bloomfield, indeed, is far from sure that the United Kingdom was always, or regularly, a net short-term creditor. As for long-term lending, a rise in London rates might very well discourage new flotations, although no one believes that any such response could have been at all speedy.

Finally, it is possible [64] that when interest rates rose all across Europe, financiers interpreted the increase as a sign of coming trouble, and moved funds from markets they thought more risky to markets they thought less risky. If so, the Romanians, for instance, would move funds from risky Bucharest to less risky Berlin, while the Germans moved funds from Berlin to still less risky London.

In short, Bank Rate seems to have worked chiefly by inducing various inward flows of short-term capital. These are called 'accommodating capital flows' because they are induced responses to a loss of gold which other forces — the trade balance, the export of long-term capital — are producing. The task was made easier by the enormous strength of Britain's current account. Even so, given the small Reserve, large speculative movements against the pound might have defeated the Bank. But no one could imagine that the pound might leave gold, or vary in value against gold. Here, as so often in monetary affairs, confidence was self-fulfilling.

It is now generally believed that at least in the short run the movements in the Reserve had little to do with the movements in the money supply. Goodhart [42], using modern statistical techniques which earlier generations could not apply, finds that in the United Kingdom the money supply varied chiefly on the basis of the 'state of trade'. The banks, having opened lines of credit for their customers, found these lines more fully taken up when business was good, so that the banks would automatically be creating more deposit money. They might also increase the old-established lines of credit. As the quantity of money increased the reserve positions of the banks would worsen, partly because gold sovereigns and half-sovereigns would leak out of bank tills and into circulation, and partly because the total of bank liabilities would be rising in relation to the remaining holdings of gold and other liquid assets. The banks would respond by reducing their supply of credit to London's money market, where interest rates would accordingly rise, thus pulling short-term funds into London whether or not the Bank chose to manipulate Bank Rate. The resulting capital inflow would obviate the strain on the exchanges which the domestic monetary expansion would otherwise have entailed, so that the Bank, and Bank Rate, would have less to do.

Britain's institutions and practices were unknown outside Europe, and even on the Continent they were anything but widespread. Crossing the Channel from London to Paris we seem to enter a much simpler financial environment, although this impression may reflect the state of research on French financial history. France was an immensely important exporter of long-term capital funds, but as a focus for world monetary flows she counted for rather little and, unlike Britain, she was normally a large importer of gold not only for coin but for additions to reserves. From January 1900 to January 1913 the Banque de France increased its specie reserves by 37.5 per cent [98, *Table 49*]. The Banque did not systematically manipulate its lending rate in response to the movements of gold, partly because it was not legally obliged to maintain any particular level or proportion of 'gold cover' for its notes. Indeed, 'Banque Rate' remained at 3 per cent for extraordinarily long periods, during which there was considerable fluctuation in the Banque's specie holdings. But the Banque was not completely unresponsive to such fluctuations. An increase in Banque Rate was 'an advertisement . . . . permitting one to appreciate the dangers of the situation, and could inspire thoughts in businessmen and capitalists'; it might also prevent funds from leaving France, or attract money to Paris [22, *41-2*]. Because five-franc silver coins were unlimited legal tender in France, the Banque could and sometimes did protect its gold by paying silver for its notes. It might also employ some of the 'gold devices' which the Bank of England used. But it abstained from open market operations, and its role in the granting of credit, except in times of stress, appears to have been 'purely passive' [98, *198*].

Then why did the gold standard work for France? What mattered was the strong current account combined with enormous gold holdings, both in Banque reserves and in hand-to-hand circulation.

External gold drains were short-lived and easily handled; internal drains, though often longer sustained, posed no threat to the mechanism; the domestic money supply was insulated by Banque policy, and by variations in Banque reserves, from the inward and outward movement of gold.

The Russian ruble was not in demand internationally, and compared with London or Paris the domestic financial system was unsophisticated and ill-developed. Russia, which had adhered to the gold standard only in 1897, was a gold producer whose current account was normally in deficit. Capital imports normally covered both the current-account deficit and the build-up of gold holdings; the State's own external borrowings could often be timed so as to obviate any difficulties, as in 1905–6. The State Bank held very large gold and foreign exchange reserves — generally far larger than the currency law required in support of the paper currency. Thus the Bank could accept with equanimity the occasional loss of gold, and although it did vary its lending rates roughly in line with Berlin and London, it generally tried to insulate the domestic monetary scene from gold movements [28]. In addition, Russian banks held considerable balances in Paris and London; these could take some of the strain in difficult periods, and could be rebuilt in happier times. The main exception to this story occurred in 1905–6, when the joint impact of the Russo-Japanese War and the subsequent 1905 revolution imposed extraordinary strain on the balance of payments.

Although Germany was an exporter of capital the process of long-term capital export was under close regulation, so that it cannot often have strained the balance of payments, the current account of which was normally in surplus. In managing its domestic financial system the Reichsbank was more active than the Banque de France, and it kept a close eye on what London was doing. Seeger has argued [90, 29] that the Reichsbank managed its discount rate on the basis of its uncovered note issue and of the ratio between note issue and gold reserves. Thus when the uncovered note issue and the ratio tended to rise, the discount rate would also rise, and conversely. 'Gold devices' were also employed from time to time. A gold outflow would tend to push the rate up. However, a gold-inflow would not necessarily bring the rate down; it might merely make the Reichsbank more comfortable about a stable or rising note issue. The economic growth of the country required a rising money supply, implying more gold for circulation and for reserves. Gold would flow in, accommodating the rise in the money supply, partly because the Reichsbank kept its discount rate above the French and British rates, a part of the current account surplus being used to finance the acquisition of gold. Furthermore, because Berlin was a monetary centre for much of central and south-eastern Europe, it is to be supposed that many of the mechanisms which were at work in Britain were also at work in Germany [25].

In much of the overseas world things were much simpler. Japan had possessed a central bank since the mid-1880s, and had been on the gold standard since 1897. To manage the exchanges the Bank of Japan held gold and foreign exchange reserves, largely in London, but because the local financial system was undeveloped it could not use the methods of London, Paris or Berlin to attract or repel gold [1, 54–60]. For India, which had no central bank, it was the government which maintained London balances and which bought and sold rupees and sterling so as to keep the rupee pegged [57]. For the British dominions, which also lacked central banks, the commercial banks played this role [41; 96]. In the dependent empires which were then attached to Britain, France, Germany, Holland, Belgium, Denmark and the United States, a variety of monetary devices generally kept local currencies pegged to metropolitan ones without the use of local gold standards or local central banks; as with India and the British dominions, the key role was played by exchange reserves held in the metropoles [57; 96]. In Latin America, however, things were anything but simple, and the arrangements were too various and too changeable to be described here. Perhaps the most interesting country is Argentina, a prosperous land where, after the adoption of the gold standard in 1899, very large gold reserves were built up by the government agency which was charged with ensuring that the paper currency would remain gold-convertible. A separate institution, the Bank of the Nation, had power to rediscount commercial bills, but it does not appear to have done so. Nor was there anything corresponding to London's Bank Rate. The Bank of the Nation, like the American Independent Treasury, could and did try to manage domestic credit by moving gold into and out of its own vaults. But as in the United States, the object was management for the sake of domestic borrowers, not for the sake of the gold standard. Indeed, the effect of the Bank's actions was to nullify, in whole or in part, the contractionary pressures which seasonal gold-outflows would otherwise have produced. Such transactions were effective because the Bank was a very large part of the banking system. But in addition the Argentine contained several British-owned banks, such as the London and River Plate, most of which functioned in relation to the London financial community in the same way as the Australasian banks within the British Empire [37, *96–105*; 51, *130–1*].

(vi) THE GOLD STANDARD AND INTERNATIONAL TRADE

In principle, because of the first two automatic servo-mechanisms which were described earlier in this chapter — the price-specie-flow mechanism and the income-adjustment mechanism — the gold standard might have produced great swings in prices, profits, employment and prosperity. In practice it does not seem to have done so, partly because periods of boom affected most of the comparatively prosperous countries more or less together, and partly because of external reserves and induced capital flows, which reduced the amount of work which the servo-mechanisms were called upon to perform, especially in the short run. Those who adhere to the monetary approach to the balance of payments dispose of all such disturbances by assumption; in particular, it is assumed that international markets for commodities and finance are so well integrated that no one country can experience disturbances; rather, monetary disturbances produce gold flows without disrupting anything else. Business cycles there certainly were, but these do not seem to have been correlated with gold movements; except when disturbed by circumstances peculiar to one country and not related to gold — Canada's settlement boom after 1900, or the Australian troubles of the 1890s — prices and prosperity seem to have moved in much the same way, most of the time, throughout the gold-standard world. In some debtor countries there were occasional stresses and strains which could be traced to the gold standard. But it was common, especially in Latin America, to deal with stress by jettisoning the standard. Hence Keynes and other critics [58, *159-60*, *172*] have surely exaggerated the damage which came from the standard, as opposed to other misfortunes —

war, revolution, unwise government policy, extended periods of external borrowing for foolish purposes. Keynes, of course, objected to the automatic features of the gold standard. But as we have seen, even in the central group of lending countries the machinery was not as automatic as Keynes thought. Nor is there any reason to deny that the gold standard and respectable economic performance could co-exist, and commonly did. On the other hand, there is no reason to suppose that a gold standard, in and of itself, could improve economic performance. When the cry for 'a return to gold' goes up, as it sometimes does in the United States, it usually comes from folk who know little about the history of the subject.

Yet the mechanism of the gold-standard system was very delicately balanced. Given the dependence on new gold for monetary expansion and for the growth of coin and reserves, trouble would ensue if the production of new gold were to diminish, as historical experience suggests it was sooner or later bound to do. Given the importance of long-term capital exports for balancing the accounts both of debtors and of creditors, any interruptions to that flow would also cause trouble, as both Argentina and Canada discovered in 1913–14. Given the almost universal need to offset deficits in some directions with surpluses earned or borrowed in others, the system could not survive any disruption of multilateral settlement. Furthermore, the trading patterns which underlay the surpluses and deficits were to some extent artifacts, reflecting as they did not only the existing pattern of trade-specialisation but also the tariff structure of the world. New specialisations, new export capabilities or new tariffs, could readily disrupt the pattern of multilateral payments, creating new deficits and new surpluses which spontaneous flows of long-term capital might or might not offset.

Much of the above was recognised by 1914. But for Britain there was another risk, which was quite invisible and not at all understood. Everyone knew that British credits financed much of world trade. Some British observers thought that the gold reserves in the Bank of England were uncomfortably small in relation to potential pulls from other countries — especially, in 1907, from the USA. But little attention was paid to Britain's large and growing short-term obligations, which no one was concerned to measure or weigh. Nor was it clearly seen that these debts were growing much more rapidly than the Bank's gold reserve, so that the liquidity position of the 'world's banker' was worsening. So long as world trade and payments remained centred in London, and so long as the world had confidence in the gold-convertibility and exchange-convertibility of the pound sterling, this did not matter. But already, by 1914, the seeds of the troubles of 1929–31 had been planted in London.

## 2 Off and On and Off Again: The Distressful Changes of 1914–1931

### (i) 1914–1918: THE COLLAPSE OF THE GOLD STANDARD

With the outbreak of war in 1914 the gold-standard system quickly collapsed because one country after another took independent, unco-ordinated actions which in combination had the effect of dismantling that system: ending the gold-convertibility of paper currency; controlling and managing the international movement of gold, either formally or in other ways; breaking links between gold reserves and currency-circulations; drawing gold coin into official reserve holdings and replacing it by paper currency (for a detailed account of these and latter developments, see [67]; see also [30]). The assortment of such steps, and the dates of their introduction, naturally varied as between countries; furthermore, it was common to retain the pre-war theoretical 'gold contents' for the various national monies. Freed from the constraining limits of the gold points, and responding to a much-altered pattern of international payments, exchange rates moved away from their pre-war, gold-determined, par values, although during the war most Allied and neutral exchange rates remained quite close to their pre-war dollar parities. All the belligerents were obliged to embark on domestic monetary expansion, though at differing rates, soon facing inflationary pressures of a magnitude unknown since the French Revolutionary and Napoleonic wars. The flows of private credit, both short-term and long-term, were much reduced, and no longer moved in the old ways. Governments — not only the chronic borrowers of pre-war years, such as the Russian Empire, but countries such as Britain and France which had in peacetime been large capital exporters — were obliged to borrow abroad for war purposes, both from one another and from American nationals and the United States government. Because the warring states found their import needs rising while their export potentials were falling,

29

gold flowed from them to the neutrals, transmitting the monetary expansion and the inflationary pressure, which became a world-wide phenomenon.

As the war continued, the external positions of the belligerents were much changed. The network of war debt which connected the Allies with one another and with the United States now seemed to be a permanent part of a world financial landscape on which the American economy and its financial system loomed far larger than before the war. The Bolshevik revolution of 1917 quickly led to the expropriation of foreign property in Russia, and to the repudiation of the Tsarist government's external debts, most of which were owed in Britain and France. Both France and Britain sold some of their citizens' assets in the United States, although most British external assets, with the exception of the Russian ones, remained intact [76, 74–5]. After the end of the war came the sequestration of Germany's external assets, which were transferred to the Allies, and the imposition of reparations payments on the former Central Powers. The United States did not share in these, but all the European Allies hoped and expected to do so. The development of new tariff barriers and new competition in many places, not least in the 'successor states' of central and south-eastern Europe and in India, plus the political changes in Russia, would make it impossible to restore post-war trade along pre-war lines.

Inflation did not end with the war. Indeed, in much of continental Europe it would continue, and accelerate, well into the 1920s, as governments wrestled with disastrous budgetary positions which the aftermath of war and the new territorial arrangements had exacerbated. In such a situation exchange rates naturally drifted ever further from their pre-war levels. Also, the end of the war brought still more floating of currencies, as both Britain and France abandoned their wartime arrangements for pegging to the US dollar at a figure somewhat below the pre-war level.

## (ii)  Post-war Attempts to Stabilise Exchange Rates

It was generally thought that the world should get back to fixed exchange rates as soon as possible. But only the United States, which went back to gold in June 1919, could quickly take restorative action. Given the state of affairs in continental Europe, where floating rates co-existed with domestic inflation, budgetary disorder, and the uncontrollable movement of 'hot money' — short-term capital funds fleeing from country to country — it was inevitable that observers would associate monetary and budgetary chaos with floating rates. Fixed exchange rates, on the other hand, were associated with the more orderly pre-war world, and often with a revival of world trade and finance. Although various alternatives were canvassed among specialists from time to time, the bankers and officials of the western world never really considered fixing rates on any basis other than gold. As a temporary expedient a country might peg its money to another money, opting for what was called 'de facto stabilisation'. Germany did this in 1923, and France in 1926. Colonial currencies, such as those in the British African empire, were normally managed in this way. But an independent and self-respecting nation would want what was called 'de jure stabilisation' — the pegging of the currency not to another money, but to gold along pre-war lines.

Before 1914 each nation's gold standard had been a matter for that nation alone, and there had been no international concertation of the 'system'. Departures from gold during wartime had been equally unco-ordinated, and so would be the 'return to gold' during the 1920s, even though monetary matters were canvassed at two international gatherings — the Brussels Conference in 1920, and the Genoa Conference two years later. Although some government officials and central banks, such as those of the United Kingdom, took these gatherings with great seriousness, the conference resolutions were anodyne, and of course they were without force or effect. At best, it might be supposed, they strengthened the wills of politicians, officials and central bankers. Budgets should be balanced, it was resolved. The issue of unsecured paper currency should end. Countries should stabilise their exchange rates, returning to the gold standard, though not necessarily at the 1914 gold parities. Gold should be 'economised': countries should not circulate gold coin, and instead of holding gold reserves they should consider holding foreign exchange. Central banking should spread, and should be free from political manipulation. Artificial exchange controls should be abandoned or avoided; central banks should co-operate, and should hold a conference (17; 86, *153–63 and Appendix 9*].

The conference of bankers never took place, although the Bank of England, which had become much more internationally minded than before the war, and which was specially anxious to see a general return to gold, did try to summon it. Nevertheless, largely under British leadership in Europe and American guidance overseas, new central banks were set up. Also, central bankers did co-operate more closely in the 1920s than ever before [15]. The Bank of England and the other central banks, including the Federal Reserve Bank of New York — the flagship of the American central banking system which had begun work only at the end of 1914 — could provide advice, encouragement and sometimes interbank credits. Some credits, furthermore, flowed as a result of League of Nations' efforts to stabilise certain economies, such as the Austrian [66; 70; 95]. Contacts among central bankers could become quite intimate, as among the Reichsbank, the Bank of England, and the 'New York Fed' [13; 18; 86]. But if central bankers distrusted one another, relations could be difficult [74].

Although international conversations could help to establish a common mind with respect to the gold standard, the critical decisions would have to be taken in each country, separately, with very imperfect knowledge, and in situations where every action was fraught with potentially disastrous political repercussions. Technical economic and statistical analysis, though developing fast, could provide only the most general guidance, and economists, as usual, did not all speak with a single voice. Nevertheless, from 1919 through 1928 we see efforts to stabilise most currencies, sometimes *de facto* and sometimes *de jure*. Germany and France began with the former and moved on to the latter; Britain, in 1925, and the British Dominions, opted for *de jure* stabilisation from the first, although they generally imposed regulations which ensured that only large sums of paper currency could be presented for gold-conversion. Roughly speaking, those countries which had experienced comparatively little inflation and which had quickly ended it, such as Britain, were able to retain the same 'gold contents' as in 1913, thus achieving the same dollar exchange rate as in pre-war days; those which had experienced much more serious and prolonged inflation, such as France, Germany, Austria [66], and the Soviet Union [10; 52], had to choose much lower 'gold contents', or to introduce entirely new currency units.

## (iii) The Reconstruction of the Gold Standard, 1919–1928

Stabilisation logically involved two decisions: one as to the date of the action, and one as to the rate of exchange. Some observers [21] were not much concerned about the choice of rate because they thought that adjustment problems would be transitory; others thought that because prices, costs and government arrangements had all become more rigid since 1914 such adjustments might happen only slowly, painfully or not at all. For many countries there is now an extensive literature on these topics which we cannot scrutinise here. Some countries, such as Britain and Canada, were never in any doubt as to rate, and committed themselves as to timing some months or years in advance. British attitudes have been thoroughly researched within the past fifteen years, on the basis of archival evidence not previously available, by Moggridge and Howson [47; 72]. Other countries, such as France, Germany and Italy, chose rates through some mixture of politics, arithmetical convenience and the desire to win competitive advantage or to demonstrate political prowess, but chose to act in the heat of the moment [19; 25; 43; 53; 63; 80; 81; 86; 87; 101]. For all these countries the research of the past decade or more has clarified the nature of the decisions that were taken.

In these circumstances a move back to fixed exchange rates was bound to be a fumbling and uncertain one, and there was a real risk that a country would get the 'wrong' rate — one which would create subsequent problems of adjustment, whether in the domestic price level, the level of employment, the current account of the balance of payments, or some mixture of these three. Given the large economic and financial changes which had occurred since 1914, no one could readily forecast what any particular rate, or set of rates, would do to international trade and finance. Hence no one should be surprised to find that the results, in relation to the United States dollar, could appear to be inappropriate. Nor is it surprising that economic historians are still debating the rightness of each such decision [72; 79; 86; 87], and wondering why adjustments in prices, employment and prosperity were not complete or speedy enough to eliminate later strain. To some extent the servo-mechanisms did work: for instance, unemployment rates tended to be comparatively high among the countries which had trouble retaining gold, such as Britain and Germany, while those to which gold was flowing, such as France, tended to enjoy boom conditions, and, in some instances, inflation as well [79; 101]. But in that many central banks did not follow the 'rules of the game' the servo-mechanisms could not be expected to work very well. Nor would they have long to do so, before other disturbances — most importantly the slump which began in 1928–9 — would interfere with the adjustment process.

By 1928, when France stabilised the franc *de jure*, most of Europe and the British Empire could be said to be 'on gold', as could the United States, Canada and some Latin American states. Even the Soviet Union gave a theoretical 'gold value' to the new ruble which replaced the disastrously depreciated old one. The reconstructed gold standard differed formally from pre-war arrangements in two respects. In few countries did gold coin circulate; in most countries the authorities would sell gold only in large amounts. Hence the common appellation: the 'gold bullion standard'. There were also two changes which should probably be seen as differences in degree: monetary authorities were rather more likely to hold foreign exchange reserves, either as supplement to gold reserves or as replacement for them; in that more countries were pursuing purposive monetary policies, the links between domestic credit conditions and gold movements may very well have been weaker than before the war. Also, because of what had happened since 1914, people were much more likely to be uncertain about the ability of any government, except that of the USA, to sustain its chosen exchange rate and to maintain gold-convertibility. Fortunately the South African mines were still churning out new gold, though rather less than before the war.

(iv)  PROBLEMS OF THE RECONSTRUCTED GOLD STANDARD

In Britain and Europe by the late 1920s the legacy of currency-stabilisation was in most respects uncomfortable, partly because countries had committed themselves to inappropriate exchange rates. The pound is generally thought to have been given a value which was too high in relation to the American dollar, given the price levels in Britain and in the United States [56; 72]. Recent research has confirmed that verdict [79], although the extent of the error is still uncertain, and it has been suggested that the mistake may not have damaged Britain's trade very much, partly because so many Empire currencies were pegged to the pound sterling and partly because France, stabilising after Britain, might well have chosen a still lower value for the franc if Britain had fixed the pound at a figure lower than $4.86 [87]. It has also been suggested [78] that the British Empire countries had something to do with the timing of the Mother Country's return to gold. The franc was certainly given a value which produced a very large current-account surplus; because French citizens were now unwilling to make long-term foreign investments and French governments were not anxious to see them do so, the surplus piled up first as short-term claims on London and then as gold. Britain resumed her pre-war role as an earner of current-account surpluses and as an external lender both on short term and on long term, but her short-term obligations, most obviously to France but also to Empire countries and to other authorities and persons which kept their foreign balances in the form of claims on London, grew. The New York financial market represented a new kind of competition, one which could pull short-term funds from Britain and Europe much more readily than before 1914. As a result the Bank of England, in its Governor's words, was 'under the harrow' from 1925 to 1931 [86, *211*]. Germany emerged from its hyperinflation in 1923 with a new unit of account, pegged to the dollar at the same rate which had applied to the old mark of 1914, even though the war had worsened the country's basic balance of payments position: external assets and ships had been stripped away, reparations payments had been imposed, and the markets of Eastern and South-Eastern Europe were less open than they had been. Hence it is hardly surprising that for the rest of the decade the nation ran a current-account deficit. It covered this, and raised the funds to make reparations payments, by external borrowing — two official loans to help with reparations, plus much larger sums that were raised by German businesses, municipal governments and banks. Much of this new borrowing was short-term, subject to withdrawal on short notice or no notice at all [25; 88; 89]. The same things happened in Austria, which also ran a current-account deficit, and where, in addition, the Vienna banks were anxious to re-establish their lending role throughout central Europe; like German banks, they were eager to borrow abroad on short term or at call so as to make this possible. They also raised large amounts in foreign share-capital [66]. In Fascist Italy, which stabilised the lira only in 1928, it appears that Mussolini deliberately overvalued the currency so as to demonstrate his dominance over the economy in general and industry in particular; the inevitable concomitant was a mixture of subsidy to exporters, and new barriers to importation [19; 83]. There is some dispute as to whether the Duce actually understood what he was doing; a final resolution of the question must await the discovery of new archival sources. As for the Soviet Union, which introduced a new unit of account and returned to gold in a formal sense in 1922–4, the government maintained a control of trade and payments which made the actual exchange rate unimportant.

By 1919, thanks to wartime lending and a continuing current-account surplus, the United States had become a net creditor in relation to the rest of the world. In the 1920s the surplus remained, and in most years the American gold stock grew, almost tripling between 1914 and 1930. If the United States had not exported such very large amounts of capital in the 1920s the golden tide would have flowed higher still. As it was, American gross external assets quadrupled, far outgrowing foreign claims on the USA. Even though much of the gold was immobilised by American currency law, the American position was far stronger than the British: American gold reserves were enormously larger than her external short-term obligations, while the British situation was exactly the reverse. Fortunately for the world's confidence in the pound, until 1931 no one knew just how precarious Britain's situation had become.

By the late 1920s it was normal for foreign observers, especially in Britain and Germany, to criticise America's financial posture. The American government insisted on the payment of war debts, but she kept her tariffs high, indeed raising them from time to time, especially in 1922 and 1930, thus making it hard for European manufactures to enter the American market. By 'sterilising' much of the gold-inflow, so that it did not systematically raise the domestic money supply, the American monetary authorities were often thought to be causing a downward drift not only in their own price level but in that of the world. This was the centre of the 'gold-maldistribution' argument which, by the early 1930s, would be blaming the slump itself on sterilisation, chiefly in the United States but also in France [12; 62]. This line of thought now has little support, even among those monetary economists such as Friedman [39] who blame the slump on defects in American monetary management; nevertheless, there is general agreement that American policies made things somewhat more difficult for the rest of the world (see also [35]). There was always a fear that the flow of capital export which prevented the world's 'dollar gap' from becoming critical might not go on forever [33]. The Americans, unlike the British, had had no lengthy experience of making long-term overseas loans and direct investments; as for short-term credits, an advance in American interest rates or the chance for speculative gains on the New York market could, and did, pull American money home. Such American opportunities, furthermore, could attract European money too.

We can never know exactly what would have happened to American imports and exports if American tariff and monetary policy had been different. There is no reason to suppose, for instance, that import outlays would have risen enough to match export earnings, completely closing the 'dollar gap'. But more expansionary monetary policy or lower tariffs would certainly have made it somewhat easier for the rest of the world to earn American dollars through trade, thus narrowing the 'gap' and making the rest of the world less dependent on the willingness of American businesses and American individuals to acquire external assets and to hold these assets through thick and thin. It has been suggested [31] that these arguments depend on a high American price-elasticity of demand for importables, and it has been asserted that these elasticities were small. But, regardless of the elasticities, an American tariff-cut or an increase in the American price level relative to other price levels would certainly have raised the American-dollar earnings of the world as a whole.

Without the capital exports of the USA and the UK, and without the renewal of multilateral settlement, the gold standard could not have been reconstructed in the 1920s. The weak links in the reconstructed system were those countries that possessed current-account deficits, short-term liabilities which were large in relation to short-term assets and free gold reserves, and/or governments whose prospects were uncertain. Throughout the 1920s, all these statements would have applied to Germany, Austria, and most of Central and South-Eastern Europe. Financial health, for these countries, depended on a continuing ability to borrow more, every year, in whatever form the money might be obtained. Anglo-American capital exports were essential to cover the deficits not only of such counries as Germany but of overseas territories, such as Australia, where current accounts were chronically in deficit. The United States was an enormous net buyer from many overseas lands, such as Brazil and the rubber territories of Malaya and Indonesia, which in turn were large net buyers from Britain and the Netherlands. Canada covered much of her deficit with the United States by drawing on her transatlantic surpluses. Even though new protective tariffs and politically motivated boycotts had sharply reduced Indian purchases of English goods, India still indirectly earned foreign exchange for the UK [61; 62; 63].

The world still had plenty of gold, but that gold was 'maldistributed' in the sense that the countries which had weak payments positions, such as Germany, tended to be short of it, while those with strong payments positions, such as the USA and France, had more than they could possibly need. On this continuum the UK occupied a middle position: running current account surpluses, she was nonetheless piling up short-term liabilities because her long-term capital exports exceeded those surpluses, and the liabilities were large and growing in comparison to her gold holdings. Hence the continuing and immense importance of the short-term accommodating capital movements which central banks had to try to induce and control along pre-war lines by the correct management of credit and interest rates. In the North Atlantic area such flows could certainly be induced, but it was not always easy to do, especially in 1929, when the New York Stock Exchange boom exerted a potent counter-attraction.

Nevertheless, so long as there was no major dislocation in international economic activity, and so long as the UK and the USA continued to finance the borrower countries, thereby concealing a variety of structural problems, in principle the reconstructed gold standard could have continued indefinitely. Furthermore, with the passage of time some of the inherited imbalances might have passed away, because of changes in comparative employment, wage, cost, price and productivity levels. Something of this sort certainly occurred in a later period, during the 1960s, when the 'dollar gap' of the 1940s turned into a 'dollar glut'. But in the 1920s the reconstruction of the system had barely been completed, with the stabilisation of the lira and the *de jure* stabilisation of the franc in 1928, when things began to go wrong.

## (v) COLLAPSE AGAIN 1928–1931

One problem emanated from the United States. In 1927–8 American capital outflows were of the same order of magnitude as the American current-account surplus. But these outflows then began to fall, so that in 1930 they financed barely half of that surplus. It used to be thought that this development had exported the depression from America to Germany, dependent as it was on American capital. Temin has shown [92] that the depression had already begun in Germany before the capital flows changed, in that domestic investment had already turned down (see also [35]). Balderston has traced that downturn neither to the cessation of capital inflow nor to a decline in exports but to the 'instability of the German economic system itself, especially of the capital market' [2, *397*]. Nonetheless, the German monetary system remained dependent on American funds, and the withdrawal of those funds would cause trouble. In 1931 things became still worse: while continuing to run a current-account surplus the American economy pulled immense sums from the rest of the world, so that America's capital outflow became a capital inflow.

Another problem came from the United Kingdom. With the onset of the Depression in 1929 Britain's current-account surplus decreased, while long-term capital exports also declined, but not enough to prevent some loss of gold in 1928–9, and some further build-up of short-term external obligations. In 1931 Britain herself began to run a current-account deficit, making her own basic situation more perilous still, and preventing her from lubricating the world system by pumping out long-term capital exports on the scale of the 1920s.

The break-up of the reconstructed gold standard, like its erection, cannot be precisely dated. The first important defector was Canada, which floated its dollar in the winter of 1928–9 after less than three years on gold. This action, however, reflected domestic mismanagement, not the international conjuncture, of which the repercussions can clearly be observed in 1929, when Argentina, Brazil, Hungary and Paraguay all had to devalue. In 1930 the banks which managed the Australasian exchanges were obliged by shortages of exchange to depreciate the Australian and New Zealand pounds [41; 44]. In the same year, to support the rupee, the Indian government had to borrow in London [94]. In Latin America, and in such central European states as Romania and Hungary, problems and troubles multiplied. Political events began to administer their own and quite independent shocks to confidence. In India, there was concern lest the award of internal self-government and perhaps fiscal autonomy might produce a weakening or a devaluation of the rupee. In Germany, the Nazis did well in the 1930 elections. A new plan for German reparations had been devised in 1929, and the German government was co-operating with it, partly because the scheme reduced the annual tribute. But among the knowledgeable there was no certainty that Germany would transfer reparations forever. A Nazi government certainly would not. And if Germany were to default, would the Allies continue their war debt payments, especially to the USA? Meanwhile, the financial problems of the primary producing countries, whether in Europe or overseas, were spreading to the financial systems of other countries [63]. To defend their domestic economies and their exchange reserves, countries were raising barriers against imports. There was a growing fear that some such countries might have to default on their external debts, which were largely payable in Britain. In Central Europe the borrower-firms which Vienna had financed found their markets shrinking because of the Depression. If the foreigners who had financed the Vienna banks were to become alarmed and withdraw their deposits, there would be a disastrous 'external drain'.

Among the millions of primary producers within the large and diversified American economy, there was a domestic version of the distressing international conjuncture. Many small banks had lent almost entirely to farmers so that when primary-product prices came down, so did the banks: in October 1930 a crisis began, such that 600 banks failed within two months. Such failures were terrible shocks to confidence, and they naturally had repercussions. Wherever possible Americans tried to convert bank deposits either into currency or into gold, generating an 'internal drain' of large proportions [39, *208–13*]. What would happen if Americans began to pull back their funds from overseas, producing an 'external drain' which Europe had too few reserves to sustain? For Britain and much of continental Europe the gold standard system collapsed in 1931. In March of that year, following a second domestic banking crisis, Americans did begin to pull funds back home. This recall was closely connected with developments in central Europe, where French banks were already moving funds out of Austria. In May the Vienna Credit-Anstalt bank collapsed. No one knew the size of Austria's external obligations. Frightened creditors began to withdraw funds from other central European banks, precisely when the decline in export prices was itself producing balance-of-payments pressures on many such states. No one had enough gold or foreign exchange to fill these demands, and there was no international lender of last resort from which sufficient funds could be drawn: the Bank for International Settlements, which had been set up in 1929, had only limited resources, and worked chiefly by concerting the rescue efforts of the central banks. The pressure was especially severe in Germany, where the Reichsbank's reserves had been falling since 1928. It has been shown that the cause of the German banking crisis was to be traced to an outflow of German citizens' own funds [50]. Foreigners, in other words, were not to blame. Still, the sequence of events remains reasonably clear. In June, when the German government announced that the new reparations schedule would have to be renegotiated, capital flight began. In early July, when a major German bank was obliged to suspend payment, the German authorities discovered that all the large banks had immense and uncovered obligations to foreigners. The Reichsbank's own reserves were clearly inadequate. The result was a moratorium on foreign payments — a 'standstill' of the sort which had already been negotiated with Austria. Both Austria and Germany received foreign emergency credits, but these were insufficient. Although national currency laws generally still defined a 'gold content', thoughout Central Europe the gold standard was dead, and the gold-standard system was gone, in that international transactions would hereafter be regulated by increasingly stringent exchange control.

The pressure now transferred itself to London, already rendered distressingly illiquid by the developments in Central Europe, where many of London's short-term assets were now immobilised. The

41

cause of the trouble has been somewhat disputed. Moggridge argues [72] that because the current-account had become negative as a result of a falling-off in the invisibles account, the situation had basically deteriorated, so that if there had been no financial crisis, and if the depression had continued, Britain would have been driven off gold because of the deterioration in the current account; Eichengreen maintains [9], on the basis of econometric analyses, that something else — presumably a lack of confidence — was at work, producing a financial crisis in the third quarter of the year. These positions are not really incompatible, in that Moggridge does not deny that a financial crisis occurred. Certainly the British position had fundamentally worsened, yet as developments later in the decade were to show, capital movements could keep the pound strong even when the current account was weak. The problem is to know when something would have happened in the absence of the continental developments; one cannot be sure that if confidence in sterling had been maintained, the pound would have been forced off gold in autumn 1931. As it was, on 13 July, the very day that the first German bank suspended, the Macmillan Committee [20] released the first estimates of Britain's short-term external obligations, revealing just how thin was the gold cover for these; soon afterwards, the May Committee began to press for a reduction in Britain's budget deficit, further damaging confidence. Already on 13 July the Bank of England began to lose gold for export [86, *391*], and it sought credits in Paris and New York. These, plus additional credits which the new National Government later obtained, were quickly spent. Eventually the Bank and the Treasury decided that the gold standard could not be maintained; when markets opened on 21 September the pound was a floating currency [86, *esp. 45*].

Leaving gold, the British took with them those Empire currencies which had already been pegged to sterling. Some European governments also chose to peg their own currencies to the pound. India's expatriate authorities wanted to float the rupee, or at least to devalue in relation to sterling, but London refused to let them do either [94].Thus, unplanned and unintended, but not unwelcome in Whitehall and the City, by December 1931 a 'sterling area' had emerged. For the rest of the decade it would attract further recruits, such as the Scandinavian states, Argentina, Japan, and in 1938, even France [28]. Its arrangements were quite different from those of the exchange control countries. Holding sterling in the 1930s, one could freely buy any currency, whether inside or outside the sterling area; one could even buy gold itself — but not at a fixed price. Some countries which had pegged to sterling were tempted to impose exchange control; by granting small credits, the Bank of England did what it could to dissuade them. Credits also reduced the risk of default [27, 10–11]. In such sterling-area countries as Australia there might well be periods in which foreign exchange was informally rationed [41], but no Empire sterling country imposed serious exchange control until New Zealand was obliged to do so in 1938 [44]. The Bank of England was certainly anxious to 'manage' certain sorts of capital movements, especially those which might arise because of new security-issues on the London market. But it was strongly opposed to any general system of exchange control, partly because Britain was so strongly dependent not only on trade but on the multilateral settlements which exchange controls inevitably discourage.

The events of 1931 brought an unexpected end to reparations and war debts. On 20 June Herbert Hoover, the American President, proposed a one-year moratorium for both, partly to give time for new negotiations and partly to let the financial situation become clearer. France agreed only reluctantly to defer her claims on Germany, but in August the moratorium took effect. In July 1932, at the Lausanne Conference, it was agreed that Germany would make a single final payment, and that the Allies would waive any further claims so long as a satisfactory arrangement, that is to say an abrogation, could be devised for inter-Allied debts. Although the United States government was not prepared to waive her claims, Germany paid no more, and all the Allies except Finland quickly defaulted on their obligations to the USA and to one another. Britain, for instance, made her last war-debt payment early in 1933. Transatlantic recrimination went on for years thereafter, muddying the international waters, increasing the difficulties of international financial co-operation, and causing suspicion both during and after the Second World War.

The gold standard system as reconstructed in the 1920s could survive as long as the winds were set fair, but it could neither surmount nor quickly eliminate a set of structural problems — inadequate reserves in many countries, Germany's current-account deficit, America's surplus, Britain's tendency to lend

43

long and borrow short, overvalued and undervalued currencies, confusion among central bankers, political worries and uncertainties, and chronic current-account deficits among the primary producing countries both in Europe and overseas — all causes of instability. In addition, in many nations the financial mechanisms were not working in accordance with the 'rules of the game', because domestic monetary authorities were insulating domestic monetary conditions from gold flows, while the international financial system had to transfer very large sums as reparations and as inter-Ally war debts. The slump of the early 1930s, by disrupting America's domestic financial environment, by worsening the payments position not only of the weaker states but also of the United Kingdom, and by producing a protectionist reaction which had complicated financial repercussions, made collapse inevitable. In 1931, Humpty Dumpty fell from his insecure perch; later years were to show that he could not be reassembled.

# 3 After the Deluge, 1931-1939

## (i) REMNANTS OF THE OLD SYSTEM 1928-1933

The events of 1931 were not the end of the story. Several important countries, including France and the United States, did not abandon gold during the disturbances of the summer. South Africa remained on the gold standard until the winter of 1932–3, when she was obliged by capital flight to leave gold and peg her currency to sterling. A group of European states which included France, Switzerland, Holland and Belgium, retained the gold standard in its classical form, thus becoming known as the 'gold bloc'. For some years these states also kept their pre-1931 gold parities, although all were obliged to defend these parities by means of tariff-increases, quota controls on commodity imports, and from time to time some ineffective and half-hearted regulation of capital movements, in which few of them persevered. Some other countries, such as Argentina, Greece and Brazil, changed their gold parities. In Germany, Italy, Austria, Central and South-Eastern Europe, the USSR and Latin America, there was no return to free convertibility either into other currencies or into gold; rather, these 'exchange control nations' tended to tighten their controls, especially in Germany, where first the Weimar authorities and then the Nazi regime pursued a policy of domestic economic expansion which naturally put pressure on foreign exchange reserves, because it increased import needs without expanding export possibilities. Inevitably the Riechsbank gold holdings fell, slipping from an average of RM 2,216 million in 1930 to an average of only RM 73 million — less than $18 million at the official exchange rate — in 1934–9. Elsewhere in Central and South-Eastern Europe, the world-wide depression was exerting a profoundly depressing effect on export earnings. Naturally there was no free flow of private credit to the area. The exchange control nations survived by elaborating a network of bilateral payments agreements in which earnings were collected and offset, country by country, usually by means of bilateral 'clearing accounts' in pairs of central banks. Such arrangements generally provided a limited amount of short-term mutual credit, so as to avoid the need to balance accounts daily or weekly. But the credits were carefully regulated and very limited. Anxious to trade with the exchange control countries, and hoping to retrieve at least some of the funds which had been invested there before 1931, the more liberal governments of Western Europe, while providing for the free or almost-free convertibility of their own currencies, found themselves making bilateral payments arrangements with the exchange control countries (for additional detail on the 1930s see [67]).

Some experts recognised that the exchange control states could not dismantle their regulations unless they could obtain external credits. But Britain, France and the United States were all unwilling to allow the free outward movement of long-term capital funds, and in any event no one believed that private lenders in these countries would willingly buy the bonds of Germany, Austria or such states. Hence there were various efforts, canvassed with some seriousness, to provide for credits through an international agency [49]. Nothing came of these ideas, it being recognised that neither France nor the United States would give up gold for such purposes.

The price-realignments of the early 1930s, and the exchange-rate changes of the decade, stimulated gold production, especially in South Africa [24], and gold-dishoarding, especially by Indian citizens. Also, to finance its industrialisation drive the Soviet Union began to sell more gold. The result was a torrent of new monetary gold, a development which was unforeseen and unplanned, although by 1934 it was already very visible. There was plenty of gold to satisfy America's thirst, to provide Britain with extra holdings, even to allow France, in the last pre-war year, to push its gold holdings far above the 1914 level [26; 101].

The monetary system certainly suffered from maldistribution of gold reserves, although few would now join Cassel [12] in regarding this as the cause of the depression. Gold-maldistribution increased year by year, chiefly because the American position was so very strong. Throughout the decade of the 1930s the United States consistently ran a large surplus on current account. American capital export had effectively ceased; indeed, American citizens were pulling back funds, both short-term and long-term, from the rest of the world, while after 1933 foreigners moved immense amounts to the United States for safe-keeping. Hence, and in spite of short periods of capital flight, the American stock of monetary gold rose from an average of $4,700 million in 1931 to an average of $16,000 in 1939. Even after we allow for the gold-devaluation of the dollar during 1933, we find that the volume of American gold stocks more than doubled.

Yet in 1933 the United States left the gold standard: thereafter American citizens could hold gold only for industrial and numismatic purposes, and gold exportation was permitted only on Treasury licence. Why had this happened? We must first remember that much of the American gold was not 'free gold', in that it was required as 'backing' for the paper currency. Thus the 'free gold' could be exhausted even when the gold reserves were still enormous. Secondly, we must recall that in the winter of 1932–3 the American governmental apparatus passed from conservative Republican to much more experimental Democratic control, while at the same time the nation entered the third and final banking crisis of the decade. Fearing that more banks would fail and that on taking office in March 1933 the new government would devalue the dollar, Americans sought paper currency and gold; at the same time, funds were flowing abroad. Thus on 4 March 1933, the Federal Reserve Bank of New York found that it had no 'free gold', and it asked the President to close all the nation's banks for a few days. Taking office on 6 March, President Roosevelt did exactly that, but he also suspended the export of gold and the conversion of the paper currency into gold [32; 39, 378].

Like Britain in 1931, the United States had been forced off gold, but the source of the 'drain', and of the problem, was primarily internal. Later developments were more purposive, and were also aimed at the domestic economy. Roosevelt was at first delighted to notice that when the dollar depreciated on the foreign exchange markets the domestic price level rose, thus assisting America's hard-pressed and much-indebted primary producers. Later in 1933 he fell under the influence of advisers who told him that by raising the price of gold in terms of the dollar he could produce such price increases. Therefore, without removing the embargoes and prohibitions of March 1933, he pushed up the gold price from $20.67 per ounce to $35. Congress passed measures which confirmed his power to raise the price further; he seems to have decided that enough was enough, but he was anxious to retain that power, and for the rest of the decade he did so.

American adventures spread consternation throughout the gold bloc, and also in the United Kingdom. In 1931–2 sterling had fallen in relation to the dollar and the gold-bloc currencies, with beneficial effects on British trade, even though much of the exchange-depreciation was offset by special tariffs. But by spring 1933 the pound was rising toward the old par value of $4.86, or even further, while the gold franc had now appreciated in relation to the dollar. The same was true of the other gold countries and, formally at least, for the exchange control countries as well, because most of them had retained theoretical 'gold contents' for their currencies.

## (ii) The World Monetary and Economic Conference, 1933

Matters came to a head in June and July 1933 at the World Monetary and Economic Conference. First suggested by American President Herbert Hoover, who was anxious to raise the world price level, the conference had acquired a large formal agenda with respect to tariff reduction and the world monetary system, plus an informal but important agenda with respect to the 'stabilisation' of exchange rates. Originally both the gold-bloc countries and the American technical advisers had favoured currency stabilisation, but when the gathering was convened Roosevelt's new government had just taken office, and it saw little connection between America's monetary adventures and the Conference prospects [17; 32; 73]. Nor did it recognise any validity in the fears of the gold-bloc countries, whose governments were terrified lest destabilising speculation should spread from the dollar to the guilder, the belga and the Swiss and French francs. The United Kingdom, however, was not willing to return to gold or to peg its currency to anything in particular, and in this it was supported by all the Empire governments except those of Canada and South Africa. The former government was much worried by the domestic currency cost of servicing its external debt; the latter, although it had abandoned gold and pegged to sterling a few months before, still thought of the gold standard as natural and normal [17; 27].

The formal conference proceedings were paralleled by private conversations among statesmen and bankers, which were meant to provide at least for exchange-rate stability during the conference itself, and for measures to protect the Continental gold currencies against destabilising speculation which might force them off the gold standard. Although the conference had not been called for the purpose of pegging exchange rates, for the gold-bloc countries that question quickly became paramount, and when Roosevelt refused to consider any concerted action with respect to the exchanges they reaffirmed their own attachment to the gold standard.

## (iii) NATIONAL POLICIES AFTER 1933

Having been forced off gold, Britain soon discovered that a floating currency had its advantages. Credit could be kept cheap and plentiful so as to speed domestic recovery both at home and in the Empire; sterling could be kept cheap for the sake of the export trade, in so far as market forces did not spontaneously hold it at a sufficiently low level [47; 48]. Such manipulation had not been envisaged in September 1931, but by spring 1932 it had become a routine matter. At the Ottawa Conference in summer 1932, when the Empire countries met to consider matters of trade and monetary policy, the United Kingdom publicly affirmed its commitment to cheap and easy credit and to stable exchange rates within the Empire, while avoiding any commitments with respect to gold, inflationary finance or any larger projects for the stabilisation of the exchanges. In these matters the Empire countries followed Britain's lead. In particular, it was noted that there could be no general international monetary standard until commodity prices had been raised, the great nations of the world had agreed to a framework for reconstruction, and the problems which had destroyed the old gold standard had been cleared away. At the World Conference of 1933, when there was fear among some dominions that Britain might align herself with the gold bloc, Britain and the Empire countries issued a new declaration which re-emphasised the Ottawa policy [27; 86, *Appendix 26*]. Until the outbreak of war the pound sterling floated, its level managed by the British authorities and pegged from time to time, while almost all Empire currencies, pegged to the pound, floated along with it.

Although the European gold-bloc countries were not, in the event, forced off gold in 1933, their position became ever more difficult, because the realignment of the dollar and the pound amounted to an upward movement in their own currencies, measured against those two currencies. The governments of such countries as France, furthermore, were anxious to avoid the draconian measures of the exchange control states. Capital exodus, therefore, was always a risk. In April 1935 the Belgian currency was devalued against gold by 28 per cent, and the Latvian currency by 42 per cent in May. For France matters came to a head with the installation of Blum's *bloc populaire* government in 1936. The new administration acquiesced in a series of domestic developments which produced a considerable inflation, raised production costs and frightened French capitalists. Unwilling either to devalue on its own or to introduce exchange control, in summer 1936 Blum was obliged to approach Britain and the USA. If the franc were to be devalued, might there be an international agreement which would stabilise the franc, pound and dollar, while protecting the devalued franc against Anglo-American retaliation [16; 26]?

In Washington this seed fell on fertile ground, because the Americans had become anxious to achieve a *de facto* stabilisation of currencies, and since late 1933 had been importuning Whitehall to that end. In London, however, there was more disquiet. Although the Bank and some treasury officials were anxious to stabilise exchange rates and perhaps to return to gold, other officials and the Chancellor of the Exchequer would stand for no such thing. After complicated trilateral talks the three governments came to an understanding, and in September 1936 each government issued a declaration, the terms having been agreed in common. Britain and America said they would not retaliate if France devalued; France said she would reduce her dependence on protective devices, especially quotas; the three governments promised to collaborate, to consult and to welcome the adherence of other nations [86, *Appendix 28*]. There followed a wave of new devaluations, as the Dutch, Swiss, Italian, Latvian and Czech currencies were realigned. By November 1936 there was little left of the 'gold bloc'. Subsequently the British, American and French central banks made joint arrangements for the common management of the exchanges, arranging to settle their mutual obligations, day by day, in gold.

The three declarations of September 1936 quickly came to be called the 'tripartite stabilisation agreement', a label which prompts the historian to recall the old jibe about the Holy Roman Empire —

not holy, not Roman, not an Empire. It should be noticed, in particular, that no country had made commitments about the exchange rate or the price of gold. When first the franc and then the pound came under pressure in later months, consultation was spasmodic, incomplete and absent-minded. France entered almost at once on eighteen months of extreme monetary confusion, propelled in part by her domestic political situation. Sometimes the franc was supposed to be held within a range of gold contents; sometimes it was a floating currency; sometimes it was pegged more or less securely to sterling; always its tendency was downward, as French inflation continued and as French capital fled. At length, early in May 1938 the franc reached a value in relation to the pound which the French authorities were able to hold. But they did not support it in relation to the dollar, and when the dollar value of sterling began to decline during summer 1938, the franc depreciated in parallel.

Ever since 1933 the United States authorities had wanted an exchange rate of at least $5 to the pound, chiefly to raise the domestic prices of the primary products which American farmers and foresters sold in Britain. Britain would have preferred a cheaper pound, but from mid-1933 to mid-1938 the British authorities generally had to work to prevent sterling from rising above the $5 mark. This they did by accumulating gold.

The strength of the pound was more than a little illusory: except in 1935 Britain's current account was regularly in deficit, and new long-term investment, especially in South Africa and in some other parts of the Empire, was continuing. What kept the pound strong was the repayment of old loans, plus an inflow of new short-term money. As in the 1920s Britain was borrowing short and lending long, but she was now also borrowing in addition to cover a current-account deficit, as Germany had done in the 1920s. In London it was realised that the short-term funds might leave as readily as they had come, and that therefore the new gold was a necessary reserve, given these new short-term liabilities.

When the funds actually began to leave, in summer and autumn 1938, the British authorities allowed the pound to slide downward, so that it depreciated about 6 per cent in the last half of the year. This movement caused great unease in Washington, which made its views known; these views were of importance partly because an Anglo-American trade agreement was under negotiation, and partly because, given the darkening of the world's political skies, it was increasingly important to make Washington think well of London. For the first six months of 1939, therefore, the British authorities supported the pound at $4.68 by selling gold and foreign exchange. In summer 1939, however, it became clear that war was highly likely. Furthermore, America's neutrality legislation prohibited sales to belligerents except on a 'cash-and-carry' basis, while Americans were not allowed to lend to countries, such as Britain, which had defaulted on their war debts. London was under severe pressure, and the authorities therefore saved gold by letting the pound slip further. Thus when war broke out in September 1939, the pound was worth $4.03, as against $5 in September 1936; in relation to the dollar the franc was barely half of what it had been worth at that time [27; 48]. Surveying these developments, one has trouble understanding why an earlier generation of scholars [61; 63; 91] thought the declarations of September 1936 had actually stabilised exchange rates.

Much of the above account has been based on archival research, using materials which were unavailable fifteen years ago. Such work has changed our view of the 1930s. First of all, we have learned not to take public statements and announcements, such as the 1936 stabilisation 'agreement', at face value. Second, we now have a much better understanding of the forces — economic, bureaucratic, financial, political — which were at work in the major states, especially in Britain, the United States and some of the British Dominions. It is now quite clear that no one was 'in charge'. There was no monetary hegemony [82], no reliable international lender which could be counted upon in a crisis. Neither France nor Germany could provide the leadership, or the funds, for a programme of monetary reconstruction. In Washington there were serious problems of a personal and intellectual sort, while relations between the government and the central bank were such that no one except the Secretary of the Treasury could possibly take much initiative, and he, in turn, was not inclined to be helpful. Although the authorities in London were more sympathetic to larger questions, especially after the 1933 conference, they were chiefly concerned with Britain's own recovery, with the problems of the overseas sterling area and, particularly after 1938, with the husbanding of resources under the threat of war. Thus in 1939, as in 1931, each nation was very much on its own [59].

## (iv) GOLD, TRADE AND THE WORLD ECONOMY IN THE 1930s

Gold flows and gold reserves still mattered, the former because they could impose painful strains, the latter because gold was still the ultimate means of settling international obligations — the hardest of 'hard currencies'. But gold did not affect the international economy or the international financial system, as it had done in the days of the gold standard. In effect, central banks had decided that it was better to take the first strain of trade imbalance or capital movement by allowing gold reserves to increase or decrease, insulating the domestic economy from such movements at least in the short term [39; 47; 48]. Gold inflows might well be 'sterilised' if and when the monetary authorities feared an excessive upward pressure on domestic credit or prices. On the other hand, if gold losses became inconvenient or unbearable, fixed exchange rates would be depreciated, and floating rates allowed to descend. Few monetary authorities would freely buy and sell gold at prices fixed in terms of their own currencies. Few governments — and not always the same governments — allowed the free exportation of gold. Hence the gold points no longer fixed upper and lower limits to the fluctuation of exchange rates.

There was little effort to manage gold flows by raising or lowering Bank Rate or its equivalent — even among those countries, such as Britain and France, which still allowed reasonably free movement of capital. This was partly because most countries, preoccupied with economic recovery, wished to keep credit cheap and easy, and partly because other considerations — worries about possible inconvertibility, exchange control, financial collapse, political disturbance, confiscation, devaluation — could and did influence capital movements much more than differences in interest rates could hope to do.

The result, a pattern of blocs and linkages, formed the basis for the wartime economy, although by 1945 almost every nation except the United States was an exchange control state. In addition, the pattern of the late 1930s conditioned everyone's thinking about post-war monetary reconstruction. In Britain and the United States it was widely believed that one could not have prosperity without reviving trade, that one could not revive trade in a world of trade barriers and exchange controls, and that one could not get rid of quotas, tariffs and controls without solving the monetary problems of the 1930s. These problems, in turn, were defined in relation to instability and depreciation of exchange rates, especially what was called 'competitive depreciation' — deliberate downward adjustment of a rate so as to gain a trading advantage. In fact, as some American and Canadian economists were already pointing out by 1960, there has never been conclusive evidence that trade and investment develop more slowly, or less healthily, just because exchange rates are not fixed. It now seems possible that the economists and politicians of the 1940s may have misread the 'lessons of the 1930s', perhaps confusing cause with effect [61; 63]. Nor was the decade full of deliberate competitive depreciation, even though some countries, such as the United Kingdom, were not eager to see their currencies float upward. The American adventures of late 1933 can be regarded as competitive depreciation, although it is equally possible to argue that President Roosevelt was manipulating the gold value of the dollar with an eye to the domestic economy [73]. Nevertheless, the design of the International Monetary Fund, as bodied forth at the Bretton Woods Conference of 1944, reflects such concerns, and so reflects the world of the 1930s [91].

In that world there was gold aplenty — production, reserves, hoarding and dishoarding, international shipment. But the gold was not well distributed for the lubrication of international trade and investment. Also, because the world had abandoned the legal and institutional mechanisms of the gold standard, the precious metal did not work in the world as it would once have done. The collapse of the gold standard can to some extent be blamed on the slump of 1929–33. But although in some countries such as Germany and Austria the defence of the standard made depression worse in 1929–31, the depression of the 1930s should not be blamed either on the presence or on the absence of the gold standard.

# Conclusion

The preceding three chapters describe the working of the international financial system between the end of the Victorian Age and the outbreak of the Second World War. The story contains several elements — international capital movements, changing trading and tariff patterns, war-debts and reparations, waves of optimism, pessimism, and speculative panic, and politics both high and low. It centres on the means by which exchange rates were kept stable, and on the circumstances which ensured that they would sometimes be generally unstable or, at least, that their stability would be uncertain and insecure. The record divides itself naturally into three parts, each treated in a single chapter.

The first chapter treats the heyday of the international gold-standard system, the years between 1900 and the Great War. After defining what people mean when they talk of a 'gold standard' and of a 'gold-standard system', the chapter explores the characteristics of the world economy which made that system function. Attention is directed in succession to those automatic servo-mechanisms which have long attracted the admiration of economists, to the structure of the world economy, to the monetary policies of the several central banks, and to the structure of international trade and payments.

The second chapter treats the Great War, the monetarily troubled years of the 1920s in which so many states tried to return to gold, and in which a 'gold-standard system' may be said to have re-emerged, and the collapse of that reconstructed system in 1919–31 under the impact of the worldwide depression. This chapter explains why the return to gold was such a chancy and uncertain business, and observes how new stresses and strains — in particular the increase in uncertainty about the exchanges, the rising and changing structure of trade barriers, the superimposition of debt and reparation transfers on the ordinary mechanism of the world economy, and the sometimes perverse policies of the increasingly numerous central banks — made the reconstructed system a fragile creature, one whose health depended to a dangerous extent on the continued export of long-term capital by Britain and the United States. It is observed that there was no period of tranquillity sufficiently long for the servo-mechanisms to equilibrate matters; furthermore, new political developments, especially in Germany and central Europe, produced additional insecurity and uncertainty, the kind of thing that Britain and Europe had largely been spared before 1914. The chapter concludes with Britain's departure from gold in 1931, the end of reparations and war-debt transfers, and the effective cessation of long-term international capital movements.

The third chapter treats the remaining years of the 1930s, when the pound sterling was floating but managed, and when many currencies were pegged not to gold but to the pound. It is observed that some countries lingered on gold in some sense or for some time, but that for some states — the 'exchange control' states of central Europe — that adherence was formal only, while for others, such as South Africa and France, it was not long-sustained. The forces which drove first the United States and then France to abandon gold are shown to derive in large part from domestic political factors and, in the American case, from disastrous developments in the nation's own economy. After discussing the continuing role of gold in the financial system of the 1930s, the chapter ends with some reflections on the connections between this system and some later developments — especially the monetary reconstruction which followed the Second World War.

The story of these years is not a happy one, and it prompts some pessimistic reflections about the international financial system. There were servo-mechanisms at work, and presumably they tended to help the system manage disturbances by itself. But periods of tranquillity were few, especially after 1914, while new disruptions, both political and economic, were common, so that the servo-mechanisms rarely had the time to do their work of adjustment. Much therefore depended upon the financiers, central bankers and politicians. But these folk only imperfectly understood the system they operated, and the politicians, in addition, were exposed to political and popular pressures which were anything but helpful. Thus as 'management' became more necessary, it simultaneously became more difficult, and success, which might be variously defined, became a great deal harder to achieve.

# Select Bibliography

In general the utility of these writings will be apparent from their titles and from the preceding text; explanatory notes have been appended only when necessary.

[1]  G. C. Allen, *A Short Economic History of Modern Japan* (1946 and later editions).
[2]  T. Balderston, 'The Beginnings of the Depression in Germany, 1927–1930: Investment and the Capital Market', *Economic History Review*, xxxvi (August 1983).
[3]  A. I. Bloomfield, *Monetary Policy under the International Gold Standard 1880–1914* (1959).
[4]  A. I. Bloomfield, *Short-Term Capital Movements under the pre-1914 Gold Standard* (1963).
[5]  Michael Bordo and Anna Jacobson Schwartz (eds), *A Retrospective on the Classical Gold Standard* (1984).
[6]  C. Bresciani-Turroni, *The Economics of Inflation* (English translation revised, 1937): for many years the standard account of the German hyperinflation in the early 1920s.
[7]  W. A. Brown Jr, *The International Gold Standard Reinterpreted* (1940): an exhaustive discussion of the period 1914–34.
[8]  P. J. Cain, *Economic Foundations of British Overseas Expansion* (1980).
[9]  Alec Cairncross and Barry Eichengreen, *Sterling in Decline* (1983): relying chiefly on secondary literature, treats the interwar period and later years.
[10]  E. H. Carr, *History of Soviet Russia* (1951–61): the many volumes contain the most accessible account of Soviet inflation and currency-stabilisation.
[11]  Forest Capie and Alan Webber, *A Monetary History of the United Kingdom 1870–1982, vol. I: Data, Sources, Methods*

(1985): an immense accumulation of fact, most of it previously available only with difficulty or not at all.

[12] G. Cassel, *The Downfall of the Gold Standard* (1936): still of great interest and value; presents the 'gold maldistribution' explanation for the depression of the early 1930s.
[13] L. V. Chandler, *Benjamin Strong, Central Banker* (1958): biography of the man who ran the New York Federal Reserve Bank for most of the 1920s.
[14] J. H. Clapham, *The Bank of England* (1944).
[15] Stephen V. O. Clarke, *Central Bank Co-operation 1924-1931* (1967).
[16] Stephen V. O. Clarke, *Exchange-Rate Stabilization in the Mid-1930s: Negotiating the Tripartite Agreement* (1977).
[17] Stephen V. O. Clarke, *The Reconstruction of the International Monetary System: The Attempts of 1922 and 1933* (1973).
[18] Sir Henry Clay, *Lord Norman* (1957): biography of the governor of the Bank of England from 1920 to 1944.
[19] J. Cohen, 'The 1927 Revaluation of the Lira: a Study in Political Economy', *Economic History Review*, new series, xxv (November 1972).
[20] Committee on Finance and Industry (the 'Macmillan Committee'), *Report* (Cmd. 3897) (1931).
[21] Committee on Currency and Exchange (the 'Cunliffe Committee'), *First Interim Report* (Cd. 9183) (1918).
[22] A. Dauphin-Meunier, *La Banque de France* (1936).
[23] Marcello de Cecco, *Money and Empire* (1974): an eccentric but thought-provoking account of pre-1914 arrangements.
[24] G. H. De Kock, *A History of the South African Reserve Bank* (1954).
[25] Deutsches Bundesbank, *Wärung und Wirtschaft in Deutschland 1875–1975* (1975): an encyclopaedic treatment of the German currency system; with its accompanying statistical volume, the basis for any serious study of the subject.
[26] Ian M. Drummond, *London, Washington, and the Management of the Franc 1936–39* (1979).
[27] Ian M. Drummond, *The Floating Pound and the Sterling Area 1931–1939* (1981).
[28] Ian M. Drummond, 'The Russian Gold Standard 1897–1914', *Journal of Economic History*, xxxvi (September 1976).
[29] M. Edelstein, *Overseas Investment in the Age of High Imperi-*

*alism: the United Kingdom 1850–1914* (1982): may perplex those not familiar with modern economics.

[30] Barry Eichengreen (ed.), *The Gold Standard in Theory and History* (1985): besides a useful introduction, contains an invaluable assortment of excerpts from the literature, including [20], [21], [37], [68] and [97].

[31] Malcom Falkus, 'United States Economic Policy and the "Dollar Gap" of the 1920s', *Economic History Review*, second series, xxiv (November 1971).

[32] Herbert Feis, *1933: Characters in Crisis* (1966): American political dynamics during the first Roosevelt year, viewed from the perspective of a senior State Department official.

[33] Herbert Feis, *The Diplomacy of the Dollar* [1950): an account of American capital exports during the 1920s.

[34] Herbert Feis, *Europe, the World's Banker* (1930; reprinted 1964): can still be relied upon for general outline on long-term capital movements before 1914, though not for numerical detail.

[35] A. J. Field, 'A New Interpretation of the Onset of the Great Depression', *Journal of Economic History*, xliv (June 1984).

[36] A. G. Ford, 'Bank Rate, The British Balance of Payments, and the Burdens of Adjustment 1870–1914', *Oxford Economic Papers*, xvi (March 1964).

[37] A. G. Ford, *The Gold Standard: Britain and Argentina 1890–1914* (1962): a careful application of the Keynesian income-adjustment mechanism in a study of the adjustment process in the two economies.

[38] J. Foreman-Peck, *A History of the World Economy: International Economic Relations since 1850* (1983): a somewhat more analytical survey than Kenwood and Lougheed [see 55].

[39] Milton Friedman and Anna Jacobson Schwartz, *A Monetary History of the United States 1857-1960* (1963): the necessary starting point for any serious discussion of American monetary history.

[40] Milton Friedman and Anna Jacobson Schwartz, *Monetary Trends in the United States and the United Kingdom* (1982).

[41] L.F. Giblin, *The Growth of a Central Bank* (1951): treats Australian monetary and financial developments.

[42] Charles Goodhart, *The Business of Banking 1891–1914* (1972).

[43] Frank Graham, *Exchange, Price, and Production in Hyperinflation: Germany 1920-1923* (1930).

[44] G. R. Hawke, *Between Governments and Banks: a History of the Reserve Bank of New Zealand* (1974).

[45] R. G. Hawtrey, *The Gold Standard in Theory and Practice* (1926 and many later editions): still full of interest, even though the picture is now thought to be more complicated than Hawtrey believed.

[46] Karl Helfferich, *Money* (English edition, 1927): a German account; with respect to the pre-1914 arrangements, full of detail not readily found elsewhere.

[47] Susan Howson, *Domestic Monetary Management in Britain 1919-1938* (1975).

[48] Susan Howson, *Sterling's Managed Float: the Operation of the Exchange Equalisation Account 1932–39* (1980).

[49] Susan Howson and Donald Winch, *The Economic Advisory Council 1930–1939* (1977).

[50] Harold James, 'The Causes of the German Banking Crisis of 1931', *Economic History Review*, second series, xxxvii (February 1984).

[51] David Joslin, *A Century of Banking in Latin America: Bank of London and South America Ltd. 1862–1962* (1963): a revealing company history.

[52] S. S. Katzenellenbaum, *Russian Currency and Banking 1914–1924* (1925).

[53] Tom Kemp, 'The French Economy under the Franc Poincare', *Economic History Review*, second series, xxiv (February 1971).

[54] W. P. Kennedy, 'Foreign Investment, Trade, and Growth in the United Kingdom, 1870–1913', *Explorations in Economic History*, xi (1973–4).

[55] A. G. Kenwood and A.L. Lougheed, *The Growth of the International Economy 1820–1980* (1983): a reliable general survey.

[56] J. M. Keynes, *The Economic Consequences of Mr. Churchill* (1925; reprinted in *Collected Writings of John Maynard Keynes*, vol. ix (1972)).

[57] J. M. Keynes, *Indian Currency and Finance* (1913).

[58] J. M. Keynes, *A Tract on Monetary Reform* (1923).

[59] C. P. Kindleberger, *The World in Depression* (1973).

[60] C.P. Kindleberger, *A Financial History of Western Europe* (1984).

[61] League of Nations, *International Currency Experience* (1944): many secondary accounts rely on this work for impressions about the interwar years, and especially about the 1930s.

[62] League of Nations, Gold Delegation, *First Interim* and *Final Reports* (1930) and (1932): embody a variety of contrasting contemporary views as to the problems with the reconstructed gold standard, and the distribution of reserves therein.

[63] W. Arthur Lewis, *Economic Survey 1919-1939 (1949)*: still remarkably helpful, although showing the marks of the 1940s in emphasis and approach.

[64] Peter Lindert, *Key Currencies and Gold 1900-1913* (1969): a mine of detail and insight, but difficult terrain except for trained economists.

[65] F. Machlup, *International Payments, Debts, and Gold* (1964).

[66] Edward März, *Austrian Banking and Financial Policy: Creditanstalt at a Turning Point, 1913–1923* (1984).

[67] P. Mathias and S. Pollard (eds), *Cambridge Economic History of Europe*, vol. VIII (forthcoming 1987): contains lengthy survey articles on the period 1870–1914 and 1914–39.

[68] D. N. McCloskey and R. Zecker, 'How the Gold Standard Worked', in J. Frenkel and H. G. Johnson (eds), *The Monetary Approach to the Balance of Payments* (1976).

[69] P. Meynial, *Créances et Dettes Internationales (Balances des Comptes)* (1926): a useful introduction to the debt and reparation questions.

[70] R. H. Meyer, *Bankers' Diplomacy: Monetary Stabilization in the 1920s* (1970).

[71] B. R. Mitchell, *European Historical Statistics* (1975).

[72] D. E. Moggridge, *British Monetary Policy 1924–1931* (1972): the standard modern account of Britain's return to gold.

[73] Raymond Moley, *After Seven Years* (1939): the beginnings of Roosevelt's administration in 1933, as told by one of the President's close advisers.

[74] E. Moreau, *Souvenirs d'un Gouverneur de la Banque de France 1926–28* (1954).

[75] Oskar Morgenstern, *International Financial Transactions and Business Cycles* (1959).

[76] Sidney Pollard, *The Development of the British Economy 1914–1950* (1962 and later editions; title varies).

[77] Sidney Pollard, *The Gold Standard and Employment Policies between the Wars* (1970).

[78] L. S. Pressnell, '1925: the Burden of Sterling', *Economic History Review*, second series, xxxi (February 1978).

[79] John Redmond, 'The Sterling Overvaluation in 1925; a Multilateral Approach, *Economic History Review*, second series, xxxvii (November 1984).

[80] Fritz K. Ringer, *The German Inflation of 1923* (1969).

[81] James Harvey Rogers, *The Process of Inflation in France 1914–1927* (1929).

[82] Benjamin Rowland (ed.), *Balance of Power or Hegemony: the Interwar Monetary System* (1976): contains many thought-provoking assertions, and many inaccuracies.

[83] R. Sarti, 'Mussolini and the Italian Industrial Leadership in the Battle of the Lira, 1925–27', *Past and Present*, no. 50 (May 1970).

[84] S. B. Saul, *Studies in British Overseas Trade 1870–1914* (1960).

[85] R. S. Sayers, *Bank of England Operations 1890–1914* (1936): the classic study of the means by which the Bank worked the gold standard.

[86] R. S. Sayers, *The Bank of England 1891–1944* (1976): an essential basis not only for British but for international financial history.

[87] R. S. Sayers, 'The Return to Gold, 1925', in L. S. Pressnell (ed.), *Studies in the Industrial Revolution* (1960); reprinted in [77].

[88] Hjalmar Schacht, *My First Seventy-Six Years* (1955): the memoirs of the German central banker who was active and influential during the interwar years.

[89] Hjalmar Schacht, *The Stabilisation of the Mark* (1927): an account by the principal insider.

[90] Manfred Seeger, *Die Politik der Reichsbank von 1876–1914 in Lichte der Spielregeln der Goldwärung* (1968).

[91] Andrew Shonfield (ed.), *International Economic Relations of the Western World 1959–71* (1976).

[92] Peter Temin, 'The Beginning of the Depression in Germany', *Economic History Review*, second series, xxiv (May 1971): argues against a tradition which claims that Germany's depression began because the United States capital flows were cut back.

[93] Peter Temin, *Did Monetary Forces cause the Great Depression?* (1976): focused on the United States, the book treats the period 1919–33, and suggests that the answer to its question is 'No'; likely to perplex all but trained economists.

[94] B. R. Tomlinson, 'Britain and the Indian Currency Crisis 1930–1932', *Economic History Review*, second series, XXXII (February 1979).

[95] J. van Waldre de Bordes, *The Austrian Crown: its Depreciation and Stabilisation* (1924).

[96] Jacob Viner, *Canada's Balance of International Indebtedness 1900–1913* (1924): one of the earliest tests of the price-specie-flow hypothesis.

[97] P. B. Whale, 'The Working of the Pre-War Gold Standard', in T. S. Ashton and R. S. Sayers (eds), *Papers in English Monetary History* (1953).

[98] Harry Dexter White, *The French International Accounts 1880–1913* (1933): an empirical examination of the price-specie-flow mechanism.

[99] D. Williams, 'London and the 1931 Financial Crisis', *Economic History Review*, second series, XV (April 1963).

[100] J. H. Williams, 'The Crisis of the Gold Standard', in F. C. Lane and J. Reimersma (eds), *Enterprise and Secular Change* (1952): a reprint of a paper first published in the early 1930s; an interesting reflection of the thought of the time.

[101] Martin Wolfe, *The French Franc between the Wars* (1951).

[102] L. B. Yeager, *International Monetary Relations* (1976): a textbook with an unusual amount of historical and descriptive material.

# Index

American: adherence to gold, 9;
banking crisis of 1930, 40;
banking crisis of 1933, 47;
capital inflow in 1931, 39;
capital outflows in 1927–30,
38–9; departure from gold
(1933) 47–8; gold stock in the
1930s, 47; monetary
adventures in the 1930s, 47–8;
monetary policy and gold-
sterilisation in the 1920s, 36;
neutrality legislation, 52;
prohibitions on gold exports in
and after 1933, 47; strong
payments position in the
1930s, 46; target for the dollar
price of sterling, 51; tariff
policy – a source of
disequilibrium in the 1920s?,
37–8; withdrawal of funds
from Europe in the Great
Slump, 46
Anglo-American trade agreement
of 1938, 58
Argentina, 10–11, 15–18, 25–7,
40, 42, 45; adherence to gold,
25
Australia, 17, 19, 26, 35, 38, 43;
depreciation of Australian
pound (1930), 40
Austria, 32, 39, 41, 45–6, 54
Austria-Hungary, 11

Back to gold in the 1980s?, 27
Balderston, T., 39
Bank for International
Settlements, 41
Bank of England, 11–12, 20–3,
27, 31–2, 35, 42–3, 50;

leadership in the 1920s, 31–2
Bank of Japan, 21, 25
Bank Rate, 21–3, 25–6, 53
Banque de France, 11, 12, 20,
23–5, 50
Banque Rate, 23–5
Belga, 48, 50
Belgium, 17, 25, 45
Bilateral payments agreements,
45–6
Bloomfield A.I., 18, 20, 22
Blum, Leon, 50
Bolshevik revolution of 1917, 30
Brazil, 38, 40, 45
Bretton Woods Conference
(1944), 54
Britain, 10, 12–13, 15, 17–20, 22,
27–30, 32–44, 46–54, 56;
barriers to monetary
reconstruction after 1931
(British view), 48–9: borrows
short and lends long in the
1920s, 35, and in the 1930s,
51; current-account deficit
after 1931, 51; departure from
gold (1931), 42, 56; difficulties
in 1929–31, 39–42; difficulties
in the late 1920s, 35, 39; gold
reserves inadequate before
1914?, 27; National
Government (1931), 42;
stabilisation in 1925, 32; strong
current account before 1914,
22
British: dominions, 18, 25, 32,
49, 52; dominions and the
gold standard before 1914, 18;
Empire, 10, 17–18, 25–6, 31–2,
35–9, 42–3, 48–9, 51; Empire

65

currencies pegged to sterling in
the 1920s, 35, and in and after
1931, 42, 49; Empire
declaration at 1933 Conference
reasserts Ottawa policy, 49;
export trade and exchange
depreciation after 1931, 49;
monetary authorities in the
1930s, 49–53; monetary policy
before 1914, 20–2; short-term
obligations before 1914, 27;
target for the dollar price of
sterling, 48–9, 52; see also the
several dominions
Brussels Conference, 31

Canada, 10, 12, 15, 17–19, 26,
33–4, 38–9, 48; dollar leaves
gold (1928–9), 39
Capital movements:
accommodating short-term
movements before 1914,
18–26, 38; and the gold
standard before 1914, 16–18,
27; and capital flight, 41–2,
45–8, 50–3; and interest rates
before 1914, 18, 22; and the
British Empire before 1914,
19; and the pound in the
1930s, 51; as equilibrating
elements before 1914, 15;
change in international
obligations because of the
Great War, 30; fear of defaults
after 1929, 40; in the 1920s,
37–40, 56; in the 1930s, 39–43,
46, 51–3, 56; short-term
movements and perceived risk
before 1914, 22; to Russia
before 1914, 24; see also
Confidence, Interest rates
Cassel, Gustav, 46
Central and South-Eastern
Europe, 35–6, 38, 40–1, 45–6,
56
Central banks, 11, 14, 20, 25,
31–2, 38, 40–1, 44, 46, 50, 53,
55–6; co-operation: before

1914, 20–1; in the 1920s, 31–2;
in the 1931 crisis, 41–3; spread
in the 1920s, 32; see also
Capital movements, Interest
rates, Monetary authorities,
and the several banks
Central Powers, 30
China, 8, 11
Choice of an appropriate
exchange rate: and competitive
depreciation, 54; and economic
performance in the 1920s,
33–4; difficulties in the 1920s,
33–4; not a question before
1914, 10, 12–13
Clapham, J.H., 20
Confidence, 40–2, 53–6; and gold
in Russia, 24; and speculation
before 1914, 12; and the gold
standard before 1914, 18; and
the pound before 1914, 22, 28;
collapse in 1931, 40–2; during
the 1920s, 36; weaker in the
1920s, 34
Convertibility of one money into
another: after 1931, 45–6;
before 1914, 11–12, 28–9; see
also Sterling area, Exchange
control
Convertibility of paper currency
into gold: after 1914, 29–34;
after 1931, 45ff; before 1914,
11–12, 29ff; in the 1930s, 43,
47
Credit-Anstalt, 41
Crisis: of 1907, 13, 20, 27; of
1929, 28, 37–40; and American
monetary management, 37; of
1931, 28, 38, 41–3, 45, 47
Currency (paper): British Empire
before 1914, 19; connection
between gold and currency
circulation broken after 1914,
30; Germany before 1914, 24;
gold-convertibility of paper
currencies in the 1920s, 32–4;
regulation of issue before 1914,
10, 20

Current account of the balance of payments: and stabilisation in the 1920s, 34; deficits – how supplied before 1914, 17; disequilibria before 1914, 14; surpluses and the gold standard before 1914, 17ff
Czechoslovakia, 50

*De facto* stabilisation, 31; and American policy in mid-1930s, 50; by France and Germany, 31; in British dependent empire, 31; in the 1920s, 31
*De jure* stabilisation, 31; in the 1920s, 32; of the franc (1928), 34, 39; of the pound (1925), 32; resultant discomforts, 34–9
Deficiencies of economic and statistical analysis in the 1920s, 32
Denmark, 25
Dollar, 10, 11, 32–5, 47–52; gap (1920s), 37; gap (1940s), 38–9; gold value of, 11, 47, 54; price of the franc in terms of dollars and price of sterling in terms of dollars (1938–9), 51–2; strong in the 1920s, 36–7
Domestic monetary management: in the 1920s more purposive than pre–1914, 32–8; during Great War, 29–30; in the 1930s, 49–55; Argentina before 1914, 25–6; United Kingdom after 1931, 49; and the gold standard before 1914, 14–15; in central countries, before 1914, 18; *see also* the several countries and central banks

Economists, 32, 54–5; *see also* the several economists
Eichengreen, Barry, 42
Exchange control, 13, 36, 41–3, 45–6, 50, 53, 56; absent before 1914, 11; after 1914, 30
Exchange rates: and competitive advantage in the 1920s, 36; and competitiveness before 1914, 12; fixity before 1914, 9ff; wrongly set in the 1920s, 33–6, 43–4
Exchange reserves, 35, 40–1; alternatives to gold in the 1920s, 31, 34; instead of gold for peripheral countries before 1914, 25
External drain, 40–1, 50–1

Federal Reserve Bank of New York, 32–5, 47, 50
Finland, 43
Fixity of exchange rates: after 1931, 45–6; and foreign exchange market before 1914, 11–13; generally desired after the Great War, 30; how achieved before 1914, 11–28
Floating currency: advantages for Britain after 1931, 49; after the Great War, 30–1; during the 1970s and 1980s, 13; rates during the Great War, 29
Ford, A.G., 15, 17
Franc: 10–11, 23–4, 30, 34–5, 48–51; adheres to sterling in the 1930s? 42, 51; and pound depreciation in relation to dollar (1938), 51; frenetic fall after 1936, 51; undervalued after 1926 (consequences for Britain), 35
France, 10, 13–14, 17, 21–4, 29, 31, 34–5, 37–8, 42–3, 45–6, 48, 50–1, 56; financial scene before 1914, 23; long-term capital export before 1914, 23; monetary policy before 1914, 23
Free gold: before 1914, 21; in USA during the 1920s, 36; in USA during the 1930s, 47
Friedman, Milton, 37

Genoa Conference, 31

Germany, 10, 13, 17, 24–5, 29, 31, 35–6, 38–41, 43, 45–6, 51–2, 54, 56; and capital export before 1914, 24; financial crisis and standstill of 1931, 41; financing of external deficit in the 1920s, 35; gold cover and the gold standard before 1914, 24; hyperinflation through 1923, 35; monetary authorities in 1931, 41; monetary policy and gold before 1914, 24; Nazi economic expansion and pressure on reserves after 1933, 45

Gold: adequacy of output in the 1920s, 34; and economic policy before 1914, 12; and support for the paper currency, Russia, before 1914, 24; and unemployment and boom in the 1920s, 34; availability before 1914, 16; bloc after 1931, 45, 48–51; bullion standard, 34; circulation a secondary reserve in central countries before 1914, 17; circulation before 1914, 10; content, 10, 29, 32, 41–2; before 1914, 10–12; in the 1920s, 32–40, 55; of monies after 1931, 45; of stabilised currencies in the 1920s, 32; of the pound before 1914, 10; dishoarding in the 1930s, 46, 54; distribution before 1914, 17; exports restricted by USA in and after 1933, 47; France, 23; glut during the 1930s, 46, 51, 53; maldistribution, 34–8, 46, 54; movement controlled during the Great War, 29; not insignificant in the 1930s, 53; parities recommended after the Great War, 31; points, 12–13, 21, 29, 53; production stimulated during the 1930s, 46, 54; redistribution during the Great War, 30; reserves, 10, 45; before 1914, 17; of Bank of England before 1914, 21; of Banque de France before 1914, 23; of Banque de France in 1939, 46; of Russia before 1912, 24; sterilisation, 36–7, 55–6

Gold standard: and economic stability and unemployment before 1914, 26–7; and new monetary gold before 1914, 27; and protectionism, 45; before 1914, 9ff; break-up after reconstruction, 39ff; collapse of arrangements in and after 1914, 29ff; countries return without co-ordination in the 1920s, 31–5; legal arrangements before 1914, 9ff; no one in charge, 20; not to be blamed for the Depression of the 1930s?, 54; really a sterling standard before 1914?, 20; reconstructed in the 1920s – how different from pre-war?, 34, and how unstable?,47; structural and institutional peculiarities before 1914, 16, 56; structural problems and weak links after reconstruction in the 1920s, 34–9, 43–4, 55–6

Goodhart, Charles, 22
Great War, 19ff, 55; see also Reparations, War debts
Greece, 45
Guilder, 48, 50

Hard currencies, 53
Holland, 17, 25, 38, 45
Hoover, Herbert, 41, 48; Moratorium (1931), 41
Howson, Susan, 33
Hume, David, 13, 14
Hungary, 40
Humpty Dumpty, 44

reconstruction and the 1930s, 54, 56

Pound, 8, 10–12, 28, 34–6, 42–3, 45, 47–52, 54, 56; depreciation in relation to the dollar in 1931, 48; leaves gold and floats (1931), 41–3; managed float in the 1930s, 49; overvaluation in the late 1920s, 34–5; strong for much of the 1930s, 51; value in relation to the dollar, 11, 34, 51

Price level: see Inflation, Price-specie-flow mechanism, Primary producers

Price-specie-flow mechanism, 13–14, 26–7, 34

Primary producers, 40, 44, 51

Quotas, 45, 50, 53, 55

Reichsbank, 11, 24–5, 32, 41, 45; discount rate, 25

Reparations, 30, 35, 40–1, 43–4, 55–6

Roosevelt, F.D., 47–9, 54; and the World Monetary and Economic Conference, 48–9; raises the dollar price of gold, 47, 54

Romania, 40

Ruble, 10, 24, 34, 36

Rules of the game, 14–15, 44

Rupee, 40, 42

Russia, 10, 13, 14, 17, 24, 29–30; adherence to the gold standard, 24; reserves of gold and foreign exchange before 1914, 24; State Bank before 1914, 24; see also Soviet Union

Second World War, 43, 55–6

Scandinavia, 42

Seeger, M., 25

Servo-mechanisms, 55–6; and gold before 1914, 13–17, 20, 26–7; in the 1920s, 33–4, 38; insufficient to stabilise system in 1920s, 56

Silver, 8, 10–13, 23

South Africa, 17, 21, 34, 45–6, 48, 51, 56; pound leaves gold (1932–3), 45

Soviet Union, 30, 32, 34, 36, 45–6; returns to gold in 1922–4, 36; gold sales in the 1930s, 46

Spain, 11

Sterling: area, 42–3, 52; tableware, 8; see also Pound

Stimulation of gold-production in the 1930s, 46

Switzerland, 45, 50

Tariffs, 53–7; and quotas after 1931, 45; and the settlement pattern in the 1920s, 36; structures affected by the Great War, 30; structures and the gold standard before 1914, 19, 27–8

Temin, Peter, 39

Trade and prosperity not dependent on fixed exchange rates?, 54

Trade barriers, 40, 44–5, 55–6; see also Exchange control, Tariffs, Quotas

Transfer problems before 1914, 16ff; in the 1920s, 34–8, 55

Tripartite stabilisation agreement, 50–2

'Twenty-four-hour stabilisation' in and after 1936, 52

United States, 9–10, 13, 17, 20, 25, 27, 30, 33–41, 43–8, 50–4, 56; a net creditor after the Great War, 30, 36; domestic problems after 1929, 40; in current-account surplus throughout the 1920s, 36; leaves gold standard (1933), 47ff, 56; returns to gold after the Great War, 30